The Macat Library

世界思想宝库钥匙丛书

解析米歇尔·福柯

《性史（第一卷）：求知意志》

AN ANALYSIS OF

MICHEL FOUCAULT'S

THE HISTORY OF SEXUALITY

Vol. 1: The Will to Knowledge

Rachele Dini　Chiara Briganti ◎ 著

苗绘 ◎ 译

上海外语教育出版社
SHANGHAI FOREIGN LANGUAGE EDUCATION PRESS

目　录

CONTENTS

引言

要 点

- 米歇尔·福柯是 20 世纪最具影响力的社会科学家之一。在知识与权力的关系这一方面，福柯拥有大量著作。

- 福柯的《性史（第一卷）：求知意志》（1976）挑战了当时大家普遍接受的关于性存在①和性压抑的观点，并提出一种理解性存在、知识和权力之间相互关系的新方法。

- 《性史》改变了学者们谈论性和性存在的方式，为一系列新学科开辟了道路，其中包括性别研究＊（性别一词是指代表"男性"或"女性"身份的特性总和；性别研究即探究这些属性如何被社会建构）和酷儿理论＊（一种文化分析方法，以承认性别认同和知识本身的不稳定性和不确定性展开）。

米歇尔·福柯其人

米歇尔·福柯（1926—1984），《性史（第一卷）：求知意志》的作者，法国哲学家、历史学家和作家。他最著名的著作包括《临床医学的诞生》（1963）（医学史研究）、《疯癫与文明》（1964）以及研究现代监狱的专著《规训与惩罚》（1975）。《性史（第一卷）》最初计划为六卷本的第一卷，研究性在不同历史阶段是被如何解读的。

对于福柯来说，他喜欢探究的是不同的知识体系的形成过程，以及知识是如何被用来控制、调节甚至塑造人们的身份。他的著作探讨了权力的本质，而权力又与知识联系密切。此外，他还讨论了知识系统如何随着时间的推移而演变。

---

① 本书将"sexuality"统一译为"性存在"以帮助读者更好地理解这一术语。

1976 年，福柯发表了《性史（第一卷）》。彼时，他已经是一位受人尊敬的知识分子，并且享誉全球。1969 年，他被任命为法兰西公学院的教授。这是一所颇有声望的法国高等教育机构，教授职位专门为做出杰出贡献的高级学者而设。福柯为自己选择的头衔是：思想体系史学家。作为一名教授，福柯每年都会开设一系列相关主题讲座。其中一个主题后来发展成为《性史（第一卷）》。福柯于 1984 年出版《性史（第二卷）》*和《性史（第三卷）》*之后不久便因艾滋病*引起的相关并发症去世。

《性史（第一卷）：求知意志》的主要内容

福柯的著作着眼于现代西方世界谈论性的方式。他在书中声称，自中世纪*（大约从公元 6 世纪到 14 世纪）以来，西方社会越来越多地将罗马天主教*忏悔圣事*（罗马天主教徒向牧师供认罪孽以换取宽恕）当作用语言来表述性行为和性欲的一种方式。这一观点违背了当时学者普遍持有的观点。他们普遍认为，过去（特别是在 19 世纪）没人讨论性，教会和国家试图阻止所有与性相关的讨论。

福柯还认为，性解放的诉求与现代社会大量谈论性话题这一事实息息相关。他的论点与他称之为"压抑假设"*的观点形成鲜明对比。"压抑假设"常被认为是 20 世纪 60 年代和 70 年代性解放嘹亮呼声背后的理论支撑。"压抑假设"理论认为资产阶级*（有钱有势的企业主阶层）压制性的自然表达并阻止其发声。福柯认为，这种观点源于维多利亚时代对性的态度（英国维多利亚女王 1837 年到 1901 年的统治期间，社会普遍存在保守刻板风气），人们通常认为这是一种被限制、被压抑的态度。

福柯将 17 世纪对性的开放态度与维多利亚时代的态度进行了对比。他认为，维多利亚时代的人们并没有完全封杀对性的讨论，而这与人们普遍持有的观点相悖。虽然维多利亚时代的人们确实试图停止对性的讨论，但在实践中却并未遂愿。这块内容是福柯分析的闪光点。他认为，在 18 和 19 世纪，与性有关的话题被大量讨论，甚至成为科学研究的对象。一场复杂的科学对话围绕性别展开，并使某些病理（即失常类型，如同性恋者 *、歇斯底里 * 的女人或自慰的孩子）得到了确认。然后，这类信息被用于定义正常行为和异常行为并为相关理论提供支持，从而促成了对性存在加以规范的法律的制定。

然而，根据福柯的说法，这种围绕性展开的话语（即讨论）接受不同的性存在并认为所有性存在都是合理的。而且，这种态度并不是由主导阶级（资产阶级或企业主）直接强加给下层阶级（工薪阶层和小农阶层）的。相反，这种态度的形成首先是为了确保主导阶级的优势，然后才在下层阶级中传播。

通过研究性史及相关理论，福柯得出结论：现代社会的权力运作并不是通过镇压或直接统治（使用武力和暴力）来强制执行。相反，权力是通过复杂、分散的技术和机制来行使对大众的统治，这其中主要包括科学或其他方面知识的生产。

《性史（第一卷）：求知意志》的学术价值

《性史（第一卷）》改变了学者们对性、性存在、权力和知识的思考方式。它提出了一种全新的有关性存在的研究方法，更倾向于历史分析，而不是精神分析 *（奥地利思想家西格蒙德·弗洛伊德 * 在 19 世纪末总结出来的治疗和理论方法，以更好地理解无意识思维）。书中还阐述了一种有关性和权力的新思考方式，为当时盛行的简单化理解增添了新的维度。

20世纪60年代，人们对性的态度发生了深刻的变化。那些支持性解放的人，以及社会科学*和人文学科*的学者们，总是能注意到个体的本能欲望与试图限制欲望的各种权威之间的冲突（这里的"人文学科"是指研究人类文化的相关学科，比如历史和文学）。这些权威可能是政府、教会，甚至是控制欲极强的父母或配偶。那些赞同这种冲突观点的人认为，只有让人们在不受法律或社会习俗阻碍的情况下追随自己的性欲，才能实现性解放。

福柯挑战了这种观点，认为性存在和权力之间的关系远比本能和权威之间的严格界限要复杂得多。在提出这一主张的同时，他创造了一种思考性和性存在的新方式，为性别和性存在研究*等新学科以及酷儿理论等新思想铺平了道路。这种新的思考方式有助于拓宽关于性的社会角色的论辩。对于研究性别和性存在的人来说，该书迄今仍是一部重要的学术著作。对于那些希望了解福柯整个思想脉络的人来说，该书是关键文本。

第一部分：学术渊源

1 作者生平与历史背景

要点 🔑

- 《性史（第一卷）：求知意志》是哲学和文化批评领域一部颠覆性著作，它改变了学者们思考性存在和权力的方式。

- 福柯曾受到他保守的成长背景和战后法国性压抑思想的影响。在20世纪60年代和70年代，他积极参与左翼运动。

- 福柯自己的同性恋*身份和自由主义*观点与他所处时代的文化格格不入，他关于性的观点与法国左派的观点也不一致。

为何要读这部著作？

福柯的《性史（第一卷）：求知意志》是对性文化观念演变的研究。该书探讨了权力阶层是如何利用性存在的概念来施行规范、控制和统治等措施。福柯认为，自17世纪末以来，西方文化中对性的讨论在不同的科学分支中得到发展，如生物学*（对生命体的研究）、精神病学*（对精神障碍疾病的研究和治疗）以及教育学*（教学方面的研究）。作为科学认知的对象，性向偏好被视为一种"真实性"问题，该问题的解决可以一定程度上揭示一个人的身份。

福柯试图回答的核心问题是："为什么我们会怀着如此的激情，怀着对过去、现在以及我们自身的怨恨来述说我们被压抑的现状？"[1]在该书以及该书之后的两卷中，福柯认为，有意识地了解、谈论性，会促进社会对性欲和性实践的理解。

《性史（第一卷）》提出了新的论点，改变了学者们对性存在和权力的思考方式。它还唤起了人们的注意力，让人们审视几个世纪以来有关性的规定是如何被用来规范公民行为和维护国家权力的。福柯提出了一种理解权力概念的新方法：他认为权力是"多态的"*，即权力形式多变，并非由单一统治者施加，权力渗透于生活的方方面面。

> "自 16 世纪末以来，'将性构建成话语'，并非一直经历受限制的过程。相反，却一直受到不断升级的鼓励机制的影响……面对一个绝不应被解禁的禁忌话题，求知意志从未停止，而是在一个不断失败的过程中一直构建着一门关于性存在的科学。"
>
> —— 米歇尔·福柯：《性史（第一卷）：求知意志》

作者生平

米歇尔·福柯于 1926 年出生于法国普瓦捷的一个中上层家庭。家人希望他可以成为像他父亲一样出色的医生。带着对这种愿景的抵触之情，福柯选择进入巴黎名校亨利四世中学，师从著名哲学家让·伊波利特*。[2] 之后他进入了法国最负盛名的人文学院——巴黎高等师范学院。在那里他在马克思主义*哲学家路易斯·阿尔都塞*的指导下钻研学术（马克思主义建立在 19 世纪政治哲学家卡尔·马克思*的思想基础上，是一种社会和历史分析方法）。福柯于 1948 年获得心理科学学位，1951 年获得哲学学位。在研习哲学期间，他曾与著名现象学家*莫里斯·梅洛-庞蒂*共事。（现象学是哲学的一个分支，研究经验结构和我们对周围世界感知的意识结构，以及感知在我们的认知方式中所扮演的角色。）

福柯曾公开表示，该书的创作不仅受其所研究的学者的影响，还受其个人经历的影响。虽然他的父亲是一位虔诚的罗马天主教教徒（罗马天主教是基督教的最大分支），但福柯并没有宗教信仰。他对宗教抱有怀疑态度，不相信宗教能完整地解释世界。这可以在一定程度上解释他对知识和权力的持久关注。也许更重要的原因是，作为一个生活在战后法国保守氛围中的同性恋，福柯亲身经历了异性恋霸权文化（一种只认可异性恋*并谴责同性恋的文化）。1948 年福柯试图自杀，后被送到巴黎的一家精神病院住院接受治疗。对于福柯后来的自杀企图，他的医生解释为福柯公开承认自己是同性恋而遭到社会污名和羞辱后的反应。

在福柯撰写《性史（第一卷）》时，他已被顶尖名校法兰西公学院聘为教授，成为法国拥有最高学术职位的学者之一。在《性史（第一卷）》出版后的第二年，他被法国政府邀请就有关强奸的法律变动提供咨询意见。[3] 在整个 20 世纪 70 年代，福柯在政治上也积极参与左翼运动。最值得一提的是，他是"监狱情报小组"*（GIP）的一员。该组织为囚犯争取权利，并分发有关监狱的信息。1984 年，福柯在巴黎因艾滋病病毒*引起的并发症去世。

创作背景

福柯《性史（第一卷）》所关注的问题，以及他其余作品所讨论的问题，都是他所在年代的焦点。虽然法国在 20 世纪 70 年代总体相对稳定，但在之前的十年中却出现过激烈的社会动荡。在此期间，法国经历了多次激烈的冲突，其中包括反战运动——法国试图通过血腥的战争来保留其殖民地，但这些战争均以法国失败告终（越南在 1954 年获得独立，但法国活动家将随后的越南战争*归咎于法国在该地区的遗留问题；阿尔及利亚在 1962 年赢得了独立）。

冲突还包括学生针对教育体系中泛滥的精英主义而组织的抗议运动。当时反资本主义 * 情绪也广泛蔓延，导致整个国家罢工和占领运动不断（资本主义是西方主导的社会和经济体系，在世界各地发展呈上升趋势，资本主义制度中贸易和工业的目的是为了私人利益）。反资本主义情绪在 1968 年的五月风暴 * 运动中达到了高潮。在运动期间，学生们占领了索邦大学，巴黎一所久负盛名的大学，以抗议资本主义制度和传统价值观。

学生的占领运动激发了法国有史以来最大规模的工人罢工，在此期间法国经济几乎停滞不前。但是，占领和罢工并没有改变法国的政治结构，这些运动最终被警察镇压。然而，这两周的动乱被视为法国历史上一个重要的分水岭。法国女权主义运动在 1968 年事件后随即兴起。法国女权主义 * 以及人们对性存在概念的关注在 20 世纪 70 年代逐渐发展起来（女权主义是指与争取性别平等相关的知识和政治潮流）。

这个历史背景有助于读者深入了解福柯作品的源起。特别值得指出的是，虽然福柯参加了 20 世纪 60 年代的许多左翼 * 运动，《性史（第一卷）》并不赞同左派关于性和性存在的观点。第一卷的目的实际上是挑战左派思想家共同持有的有关性解放的论点。人类本能的性冲动与试图压制这一冲动的国家权力机构或资本主义力量之间的紧张关系，是这个时期的讨论重点。福柯认为，这种区分被压迫者和压迫者的方法过于简单化，他试图挖掘其中更为复杂的关系。

1. 米歇尔·福柯：《性史（第一卷）：求知意志》，罗伯特·赫尔利译，伦敦：企鹅出版社，1998年，第8—9页。

2. 丹尼尔·德费尔："福柯纪年史"，载《福柯研究指南》，克里斯托弗·法尔宗等编，奇切斯特：威利父子出版社，2013年，第11页。

3. 参见莫妮克·普拉扎："我们的代价与他们的利益"，载《性的问题：法国唯物主义女性主义》，戴安娜·伦纳德和丽莎·阿德金斯编，伦敦：泰勒和弗朗西斯出版社，1996年，第184页。

2 学术背景

要点 🔑

- 福柯挑战了当时普遍用来解释性意识的精神分析方法，提出人们并不是天生就有性意识，性意识是社会条件作用的结果。

- 人们通常会将福柯与结构主义*和后结构主义*的思想流派联系在一起，尽管他从不认为自己是这两种思想运动的一部分。（结构主义和后结构主义是文化分析的方法，这两种方法在对客观知识的把握程度等相关方面存在差异。）

- 19世纪德国哲学家弗里德里希·尼采*对福柯影响极大。

著作语境

1968年五月风暴（席卷欧美的激进社会运动时期）之后，福柯的《性史（第一卷）：求知意志》开始成为学术界乃至整个社会的讨论对象。20世纪60年代和70年代，西方关于性和性存在的学术讨论在很大程度上受到精神分析思想的影响。

精神分析始于19世纪末。它最初是由奥地利神经学家*西格蒙德·弗洛伊德提出的。他认为一个人的身份是由他们无意识的欲望和被压抑的童年记忆所形成的。这些记忆之所以被压抑是因为它们并不被社会所认可（例如，对父或母一方的性欲望或目睹父母性行为的经历）。弗洛伊德认为个体的性身份是由这些经历所塑造的。在20世纪60年代和70年代，社会科学家，诸如德裔美国哲学家赫伯特·马尔库塞*和奥地利精神分析家威廉·赖希*，将精神分析概念引入他们的著作中。福柯质疑这种思考方式，并另辟蹊径，将性存在视为社会条件作用的结果，而非与生俱来的天性。

福柯颠覆精神分析思想，声称一个人的性取向*或性偏好并不是由本能和无意识的冲动所决定，而是由社会所接受的楷模或典范所建构。他写道，人们对性通常持有两种观念："异常的"和"正常的"性行为。对于福柯而言，这种区别有助于将特定社会中被允许的性行为（如异性恋和婚内生殖性行为）与那些不被允许的性行为（如同性恋和婚外性行为）区分开来。福柯认为，这些行为准则并没有自然性或普遍性可言。由于社会对"异常"和"正常"的定义会随着时间的推移而变化，对性存在的定义也是如此。换句话说，性存在是社会历史环境不断变化的产物，而不是如精神分析派所宣称的是一种无意识的冲动。

此外，福柯认为精神分析以探讨性压抑为其重点的方式不过是现代权力机制的另一个产物。精神分析可能会声称，公开谈论性有助于释放个人被压抑的经历。但福柯认为这种观点本身就是一种控制形式，与维多利亚时代的医生用来"治愈"性"变态"的方法没有太大区别。五月风暴之后的法国，人们讨论性的兴趣日益浓厚，这是当时反抗政府镇压的一种方式。福柯对这种反抗方式很有抵触，在当时的大环境中独树一帜。

> "事实上，令人费解的并不是现代社会假装性不存在，而是当人们在无休止地谈论性的同时，却又将它视为某种不可言说的秘密。"
>
> —— 米歇尔·福柯：《性史（第一卷）：求知意志》

学科概览

除精神分析外，另外两个思想流派——结构主义和后结构主义——也极大地影响了 20 世纪人文社科思想的进程，并且与福柯的作品密切相关。事实上，他的三卷本《性史》（以及其他著作）被称为结构主义和后结构主义的代表作品，尽管福柯本人反对这样的标签。

结构主义是在第一次世界大战*（1914—1918）后由瑞士语言学家*费尔迪南·索绪尔*以及后来的法国人类学家克劳德·列维–斯特劳斯*和法国哲学家路易·阿尔都塞发展起来的。阿尔都塞是福柯的老师，对他的思想形成有着深刻的影响。（语言学是研究语言的本质和功能的学科；人类学研究的是人类，特别是人的文化、信仰和社会。）这些思想家认为所有文化都是构建而成的，即文化是法律和不成文规则的产物，这些法律或规则被用来管理人们的行为方式和信仰。为了理解任何单一的文化元素，我们必须考察它所属的制度或整个社会体系。

《性史》的中心论点即性是由每个社会建构而成的。这一观点可以理解为一种结构主义的分析方法。根据这种观点，社会中的文化元素都是由这些元素与宏大思想、制度和社会体系之间的相互关系而形成的。[1] 同样，结构主义认为，性在不同的社会有着不同的表现，因为性受当时的历史和文化环境所影响。

后结构主义是在 20 世纪 60 年代和 70 年代由结构主义发展而来的运动，主要源于雅克·德里达*等法国理论家和哲学家的作品。这些学者认为，我们对社会结构和分类的理解并非一成不变，而是处于不停变化之中，在真理与舛误中徘徊不定。他们声称，因为所有人都是他们各自历史环境的产物，并且是他们各自文化的参与者，所以没有人能够"客观地"、没有偏见地检验任何事情。因此，任何研究文化产物（任何由人创作并反映其所在文化的作品）的学者都必须认识到，他们自己的处境和背景在某种程度上会影响他们的分析。所以，《性史》也可以被理解为一部后结构主义作品，其主旨是打破既定的分类并反驳看似稳定的定义。[2]

虽然人们经常将福柯与后结构主义联系在一起，但他并不是任何特定的思想流派的成员。他的历史研究方法与年鉴派＊（一个有影响力的法国历史探究学派，专注于研究历史中的社会问题而不是外交或政治问题）有关，但福柯从未明确表示他归属于此流派。

学术渊源

福柯的作品受 19 世纪德国哲学家弗里德里希·尼采的影响极大。福柯称其在《性史》中使用的研究方法——他称之为"谱系＊批判"——在很大程度上可归功于尼采的《论道德的谱系》（1887）一书。[3]

在哲学中，"谱系"指的是对一特定历史时期的不同信仰体系的整体分析，而非单个研究。谱系法不关注这些信仰体系的起源，而是关注允许它们存在的条件（例如，当时的法律）。福柯用这个术语描述了他自己的历史分析方法。他的方法假设所有的既定真理都是可质疑的，历史本身就是一个可以被无休止地修改的概念，因为每一代人都会对过去提出一种不同的观点，这种观点经常与上一代人的观念相矛盾。《性史（第一卷）》的副标题"求知意志"参考了尼采的"权力意志"＊一说。尼采用这个术语来描述人类的驱动力，即渴望获得最高地位的野心和欲望。这个术语也反映了福柯的主要目标，即分析有关了解和谈论性存在的意志是如何建构的，这一意志又是如何影响我们社会对于性实践的理解的。

福柯承认尼采是他最大的影响来源之一。他说："如果我自命不凡的话，我会用'道德的谱系'来作为我的作品的总标题。"[4]总的来说，福柯意在探究科学家如何将性存在作为求知的对象进行研究，这也同时反映了他对现代结构和制度不断提出质疑的终极目标。

---

1. 休伯特·德雷福斯和保罗·拉比诺编：《米歇尔·福柯：超越结构主义与解释学》，芝加哥：芝加哥大学出版社，1983 年；大卫·拉曼等："定位性史"，载《性存在再思考：福柯与古典研究》，大卫·拉曼等编，新泽西州普林斯顿：普林斯顿大学出版社，1998 年，第 3—41 页。

2. 尼基·沙利文：《对酷儿理论的批判性介绍》，纽约：纽约大学出版社，2003 年，第 40 页。

3. 弗里德里希·尼采：《论道德的谱系与看这个人》，纽约：兰登书屋，2010 年。

4. 艾伦·斯克里夫特：《尼采的法国遗产：后结构主义的谱系》，伦敦：劳特利奇出版社，1995 年，第 33 页。

3 主导命题

要点 🔑

- 《性史（第一卷）》挑战了学者们对性、性存在和权力的思考方式，并挑战了关于 19 世纪社会中性存在所起作用的普遍观点。

- 由 19 世纪政治哲学家卡尔·马克思和精神分析学家西格蒙德·弗洛伊德的著作所开创的理论方法，在 20 世纪 60 年代和 70 年代主导了福柯所在领域的学术思想，但福柯并没有在他的著作中遵循这一理论方法。

- 《性史（第一卷）》提出了一种考察压制和权力的新方式，反对诸如德裔美国文化评论家赫伯特·马尔库塞等学者的观点，并声称不能将权力与单一的地点或个人挂钩。

核心问题

米歇尔·福柯的《性史（第一卷）：求知意志》挑战了他那个时代知识界和广大公众对性存在的理解。这本书的核心问题是："为什么像我们这样的社会会如此公开地谈论性压抑呢？"福柯分析这个问题的方式非常独特。他提出了一种思考性存在和权力的全新方式，与当时的学术观点背道而驰。

《性史（第一卷）》旨在说明性存在并不能简单地被理解为一个社会的主导阶级（即富人与掌权者）试图在下层阶级中加以压制之物，因此正面驳斥了 20 世纪 60 年代和 70 年代许多人文社科领域学者所持有的观点。福柯质疑了他所称的"压抑假设"。"压抑假设"认为权力，无论是以法律形式还是以资产阶级（中产阶级）社会的形式，都会压抑性存在。例如，公开谈论性被认为是不恰当的，该假设还认为只有下层阶级才会不受约束地满足他们的性欲。从这个意义上说，只有当我们彻底摆脱所有这些对性存在的限制时，性解放才会真正实现。根据这些观点，权力只会产生消极影响：它压抑并扼杀本能的性冲动。

福柯不同意这一立场。相反，他认为权力也可以是积极的、有生产性的，因为它塑造了我们看待世界的方式，其中包括我们的欲望和偏好。

该书对 20 世纪 60 年代和 70 年代的社会运动提出了挑战。在压抑假设主导的背景下，这些社会运动声称他们将公众从 19 世纪遗留下来的压抑态度中解放出来。福柯认为，19 世纪人们对待性存在的观点实际上比学者们所设想的更为复杂，左翼活动家的论点过于简单，而且从历史角度看，有失偏颇。

> "（现代性*使）肉体成为所有邪恶的根源，将最重要的违法行为从行为本身转移到人心的欲望，因此难以察觉和表达。这是一种摧毁整个人的邪恶，并且是以最秘密的形式存在。"
>
> —— 米歇尔·福柯：《性史（第一卷）：求知意志》

参与者

福柯的作品一部分是对弗洛伊德—马克思主义*的批判。弗洛伊德—马克思主义是一种文化分析的方法，借鉴了西格蒙德·弗洛伊德的精神分析方法和卡尔·马克思对资本主义社会和经济制度的批判。弗洛伊德精神分析认为文化是人类行为、无意识的欲望以及被压抑的冲动相互作用的产物。马克思主义批评从不同社会经济阶层人们之间的冲突角度来理解文化。

从弗洛伊德—马克思主义的角度来看，性存在首先是压迫的工具。社会的上层阶级决定何为正确、合理，然后利用这些规范来统治下层阶级，而个人则在内心欲望与社会规范之间的冲突中徘徊。这个观点源于德国精神分析家威廉·赖希。在他的"性压抑"理论中，赖希指出压抑是资本主义剥削的必要组成部分。他强调，"强行控制一个人的性存在……会导致病态的、带有感情因素的荣誉和责任感、勇敢和自我控制等概念的发展。"[1]在赖希看来，过度压抑会使群众接受专制统治，政府权威面前将无个人自由可言。

福柯质疑赖希的观点，却对赖希极力讨论性压抑的迫切需求特别感兴趣。在福柯看来，精神病学家和生物学家用文字的形式将性存在表达出来的同时也反映了他们自身的偏见。在《性史（第一卷）》结尾处，福柯指出，"事实上，西方社会中的性行为方式可以迎来很多变化（例如，由于避孕药及其他避孕方法的流行而产生对性更为宽松的态度），而这并不需要借助赖希所预想的美好愿景及政治条件的实现。这些变化是以证明整个性'革命'与'反压抑'斗争虽有其不可否认的重要性，但也只不过是性存在的战略部署中一次战术转变或战术逆转。"[2]

福柯认为虽然性革命的重要性毋庸置疑，但同时也要认清政治左翼在说明其重要性时所给出的不同原因。他认为这是一个非常有趣的例子：不同的利益集团（科学机构、政党等）如何以发展性观念为由来促进他们自己目标的实现。在维多利亚时代，"性存在的战略部署"被用于诊断精神疾病以及制约不当行为，而在20世纪60年代，它却成为一种解除这些制约的方式。对于福柯来说有意思的是，持有相反意见的不同机构，却不约而同地利用有关性的讨论来推进自己的政治议题。

福柯认为赖希是压抑假设的最有力推动者之一。福柯对性解放或其他方面的解放的观念持怀疑态度。他的分析方法与弗洛伊德—马克思主义方法相悖，而弗洛伊德—马克思主义方法在很大程度上影响了福柯所处年代的思想论辩。福柯提出了新的理念来替代他所批判的思想。他的著作旨在展示 19 世纪人们思考性和性存在的真实情况，并且从更广泛的意义上来论证权力的运作方式并不像许多人所认为的那样。

当时的论战

《性史（第一卷）》也可以被看作针对德裔美国哲学家赫伯特·马尔库塞所作出的回应。虽然在文中并没有直接提及马尔库塞的名字，但福柯经常在关于"压抑假说"的采访中提到他。例如，在《性史（第一卷）》出版前一年的一次采访中，福柯将自己与"马尔库塞这样的马克思主义者区别开来，并声称他们将压抑的概念夸大了"。[3]

在书中，每当福柯谈到权力时，他的思想明显与马尔库塞的思想相左。马尔库塞最有影响力的核心观点之一就是"大拒绝"*概念。他将其定义为"抗议不必要的镇压，争取最终自由的斗争，以实现'没有焦虑地生活'"。[4]换句话说，要自由地生活，就必须反对一切形式的镇压，并反对由当权者来决定人的行为以及信念的做法。

与马尔库塞相反，福柯声称权力并不属于一个人或一个地方，因为人们可以抵制单一权力替身的影响。相反，权力是多维的，分布在各种关系和网络中。正如他在《性史（第一卷）》中所说的那样，"大拒绝并没有单一的关注对象，没有反抗的灵魂、所有叛乱的根源，也没有革命的纯粹法则。"[5]这一陈述清晰地呈现了对马尔库塞观点的批判。由于权力是分散的，与权力的对抗比马尔库塞理论所阐释的要复杂得多，因为对抗涉及的不仅仅是单个人（国王、上司）或单个机构（政府、公司）的权威。

1. 威廉·赖希：《法西斯主义的大众心理学》。纽约：法勒，斯特劳斯和吉鲁出版公司，1970年，第54页。

2. 米歇尔·福柯：《性史（第一卷）：求知意志》，罗伯特·赫尔利译，伦敦：企鹅出版社，1998年，第131页。

3. 米歇尔·福柯：《权力、知识：入选访谈及其他著作：1972—1977》，科林·高登等译，科林·高登编，纽约：兰登书屋，1980年，第59页。

4. 赫伯特·马尔库塞：《爱欲与文明：对弗洛伊德思想的哲学探讨》，波士顿：灯塔出版社，1974年，第149—150页。

5. 米歇尔·福柯：《性史（第一卷）：求知意志》，第95—96页。

4 作者贡献

要点 🔑

- 福柯提出了一套独特的权力理论，即权力是分散的，也是富有生产性的。权力具有建构欲望、身份和乐趣的能力，而不仅仅是压制它们。

- 福柯认为人的身体，而不是人本身，才是可以实施控制的对象。

- 《性史》原本打算成为一个六卷本系列，旨在分析性存在在各个时代的作用；第一卷关注 19 世纪的性存在，第二卷考察了古希腊的性存在，第三卷考察了古罗马的性存在。

作者目标

米歇尔·福柯的《性史（第一卷）：求知意志》旨在实现三个目标：挑战"压抑假设"；证明从 17 世纪后期开始，性就一直被视为科学分析的对象；推进关于权力运作机制的新理论。

福柯试图表明，从 17 世纪后期以来，心理学家*、生物学家、医生、人口统计学家*（用统计数据分析某个社会构成的学者）都认为性是一种"真实性"问题，即需要仔细研究、著述讨论和理解的问题。现代观点认为 18 世纪和 19 世纪资产阶级社会是压制性的，福柯想要证明这种观点与起初试图压制性存在的主导叙事如出一辙。换句话说，他认为对性压抑历史的"知识"本身就是被构建而成的："为什么我们会怀着如此的激情，怀着对过去、现在以及我们自身的怨恨来述说我们被压抑的现状？"[1]

福柯提出了一种独特的权力理论，认为权力是分散的，并不局限于某一个人或某一个地方。通过探索 19 世纪的思想家如何研究性，福柯希望表明权力不仅具有压制性，它还具有生产性，并且能够建构欲望、身份和快乐，而不仅仅是压制它们。简而言之，福柯试图定义"权力—知识—快感的机制，这种机制支撑了西方对人类性存在的讨论"。[2]

> "不应将性存在视为一种受权力制约的自然现象，或是一个由知识慢慢照亮的灰色领域。相反，性存在是历史构建的产物，是被赋予的名称。"
>
> —— 米歇尔·福柯：《性史（第一卷）：求知意志》

研究方法

福柯原来打算把《性史》写成一个六卷本系列，旨在研究整个历史中性存在的表现方式及其所扮演的角色。第一卷是六卷中的第一部。在第一卷中，福柯对从中世纪到 19 世纪的神学 *、精神病学和医学文本与实践进行了研究、比较和对比，以便了解 18 世纪和 19 世纪对性存在的看法是如何变化的。

福柯聚焦于身体，视身体为权力操控个体的场所，从而分析性存在的理论和实践背景。这种对身体而非个体的关注尤为重要。个体不再是当权者可以瞄准攻击的最基本的稳定实体。福柯希望避免侧重于权力关系中的任何一方。他强调，不仅仅是制度压迫人，而且最普通的关系也会影响制度。也就是说，并不存在行使权力的原动力或有较力。福柯说，权力可以自上而下地运作，同样可以自下而上地起作用。

时代贡献

福柯在出版了《性史》第二卷和第三卷之后不久，便因艾滋病病毒引起的相关并发症而离世，因此很难确定他是否实现了其最初的研究目标。同样不得而知的是，如果福柯完成了《性史》六卷本的撰写，我们对他的著作的看法，以及对他整个思想体系的审视，会不会大不相同。第二卷和第三卷出版的延迟（它们在第一卷出版 8 年后才推出）足可证明福柯对该研究项目失去了兴趣，又或许他陷入了某种思考上的僵局。同时，第二卷和第三卷出版的延迟也可能是他与出版商之间的问题所造成。[3] 虽然福柯只实现了最初目标的一部分，但他已出版的卷本却明显改变了学者们对性的看法。这些作品还进一步推进了他早期作品中有关权力关系和知识的讨论。

虽然《性史》的第二卷和第三卷讨论了一些和第一卷相同的问题，特别是性存在与权力之间的关系、欲望的调节以及身体作为一种社会建构的性质，但是第二卷和第三卷采用了一种截然不同的分析方法。在第二卷中，福柯考察了色情快感在古希腊文化中的作用，重点关注许多古希腊书籍中的相关描绘。在第三卷中，他研究了性在古罗马的角色，重点关注塞涅卡 *、普鲁塔克 * 和爱比克泰德 * 等哲学家对性的思考，以了解罗马帝国时期的性观念是如何变化的。这两卷都试图理解为什么西方文化倾向于从道德层面来评判性，以及为什么对性的约束远远超过对其他身体欲望（如饥饿、睡眠或攻击）的约束。

1. 米歇尔·福柯:《性史（第一卷）：求知意志》，罗伯特·赫尔利译，伦敦：企鹅出版社，1998 年，第 8—9 页。

2. 福柯:《性史（第一卷）》，第 11 页。

3. 参见丹尼尔·德费尔:"年代学"，载《福柯研究指南》，克里斯托弗·法尔宗等编，奇切斯特：威利父子出版社，2013 年，第 60 页。

第二部分：学术思想

5 思想主脉

要点 ⌖━┈

- 《性史（第一卷）》考察了自 18 世纪以来性观念在西方社会的蓬勃发展。

- 该书挑战了 19 世纪关于性和性存在的普遍观点。福柯继续考察了同一时期对性存在的科学研究，阐释了认知是如何被构建的，论证了权力具有生产性这一观点。

- 虽然福柯的写作风格让他的作品晦涩难懂，但是他在写作中通常会对读者可能遇到的问题预先提供对策，从而帮助读者理解。

核心主题

米歇尔·福柯《性史（第一卷）：求知意志》探讨了自 18 世纪以来关于性的各种观点，以及人们谈论性的新方式是如何在现代西方社会中发展和传播的。该书挑战了"压抑假设"，该假设认为社会的主导阶层（富裕的中产阶级和教会）在强调性的生殖功能时，却抑制和抹杀其令人愉悦的一面。性在西方社会受到限制，只有在同为异性恋的夫妻的卧室里，性才被认为是可以接受的话题。在这样的前提下，到了 19 世纪，社会中对性的讨论仍然受到限制。

福柯针对"压抑假设"提出了三个重要的问题：第一个问题从历史角度出发，第二个问题从理论角度出发，第三个问题从历史—政治角度出发。首先，性压抑是不是一个历史事实？是否真的有事实可循？其次，权力在社会当中是否真的通过压迫机制来发挥作用？第三，性解放的概念是不是其强烈谴责的"压迫性"权力网络的一部分？

福柯指出，在他撰写这本书时，西方的性解放诉求实际上与解放者希望抵制的性压抑的历史同时进行。他认为，与其单纯地压抑性，强权阶级反而试图让人们谈论性，并使其成为科学分析的对象。《性史（第一卷）》的主题包括：性研究与国家对性行为的约束之间的关系；性和性存在这些概念的演变过程；现代科学领域的学科在塑造我们对性存在的理解上所起的作用；以及性、权力和知识之间的关系。

> "在19世纪出现的社会，无论你称之为资产阶级社会、资本主义社会还是工业社会，并没有从根本上否认性。相反，社会投入了一整套机制来创造关于它的语境。"
>
> —— 米歇尔·福柯：《性史（第一卷）：求知意志》

思想探究

福柯在《性史（第一卷）》中提出的最重要论点是知识（这里指的是从对性存在的研究中得到的知识）、权力和身份建构之间的关系。福柯挑战了自资产阶级社会兴起以来关于性存在受到压抑的流行观点。他指出，在18世纪和19世纪，性存在已成为生物学、人口统计学、教育学和精神病学等萌芽领域内科学分析的对象。这些学科带来了关于性欲、性取向和性偏好的知识，这些方面与个人的性格特征息息相关。福柯将其称为性科学。

福柯认为，性科学所产生的影响之一是19世纪的社会开始将性与一个人的身份紧紧挂钩。换句话说，当时的社会认为性能够揭示个人的真实自我。科学家把他们认为表现出"异常"性欲或性行为的人作为研究对象。精神病人、罪犯的性存在以及同性之间的性行为也激起了科学家的好奇心。科学家根据他们在研究中获得的知识，依据不同的性取向将个体划分为不同类别。

根据福柯的说法，"同性恋"一词正是此类研究的产物。该术语于 1870 年首次出现在德国神经学家和精神病学家卡尔·韦斯特法尔 * 撰写的一篇文章中，继而成为科学讨论的对象。韦斯特法尔用这个术语来定义具有某种特征的特定类型的人——即福柯所说的"一种灵魂上的雌雄同体 *（同时拥有男性和女性器官）"。[1] 韦斯特法尔观察两个男人之间的性行为，并在此基础上建立了一套完整的理论和身份类别。和性科学一样，这种分类促进了新型监管形式的兴起，此类监管旨在遏制"异常"性行为。[2]

福柯从中得出结论，现代社会的权力运作主要不是通过直接压制（例如，阻止人们谈论他们的性幻想）来起作用。相反，权力通过知识的生产来运作（收集关于人们性幻想的详细信息，然后利用这些信息来得出定义正常行为和异常行为的理论原则，以及制定维护这些原则的法律）。福柯认为，社会的知识生产者们（分析人类行为，得出相关结论，然后将这些信息反馈给社会的机构）在影响人们的欲望和理想方面发挥着核心作用。正是在这个意义上，福柯认为权力富有生产性。我们的性行为（对福柯来说，我们的所有行为）是社会中权力结构的产物：这是福柯对社会科学最重要的贡献。

语言表述

《性史（第一卷）》中含混的措辞和复杂的论点，可能会让读者误认此书是针对学术受众而著。但正如介入学术讨论一样，福柯同时也旨在介入公众辩论。

福柯与学术界以外读者对话的努力可以被看作他思想观念面向更广泛大众的一种转变。历史学家弗朗索瓦·多斯认为，福柯20世纪70年代著作与60年代著作之间最明显的区别在于他在草根行动中的亲身参与，特别是参与监狱情报小组的成立——这是法国为因犯争取权力而兴起的组织。多斯认为，20世纪70年代最重要的"福柯立场转变"是"他亲身投入到他的理论研究对象当中"。[3]

然而，这种转变并没有反映在福柯的写作风格中。他的立场转变在帮助普通读者理解其作品内容方面几乎没有发挥任何作用。正如福柯自己承认的那样，他的观点在逐渐展开的同时，倾向于"以造成作者和读者的某种理解困难为代价"。[4]对福柯还不熟悉的读者会注意到他的作品通常假定他的受众熟悉广泛的文化现象。他的论点常常充斥着难以理解的引证，而他的动辄长达一段的长句让有经验的学者也难以索解。然而，可能会令读者感到欣慰的是，与福柯的早期作品相比，例如《临床医学的诞生》*（1963）和《词与物》*（1966），《性史（第一卷）》还是一本相对比较容易理解的作品。

福柯的另一个写作风格特点是他倾向于首先质疑他自己的论点，然后再论证、推进原先的观点。这种写作方法可以让他对读者可能会遇到的问题预先提供对策，使读者更容易理解文中论点的走向。

1. 米歇尔·福柯:《性史（第一卷）:求知意志》,罗伯特·赫尔利译,伦敦:企鹅出版社,1998 年,第 43 页。

2. 福柯:《性史（第一卷）》,第 45 页。

3. 弗朗索瓦·多斯:《从结构到解构（第二卷）:符号集,1967 年至今》,黛博拉·格拉斯曼译,明尼阿波里斯:明尼苏达大学出版社,1998 年,第 249 页。

4. 保罗·拉比诺:"序言",《米歇尔·福柯:伦理学、主体性和真理》,保罗·拉比诺编,纽约:新新出版社,1997 年,第 vii 页。

6 思想支脉

要点 🔑

- 福柯的《性史（第一卷）》思考权力的运作，并进一步推进自己的观点，指出个体身份有一部分由知识生产者所塑造。这意味着即使是那些抵制权威的人也必须在他们所反对的体制内进行抵制。

- 这一概念受到质疑，并在一定程度上被学术界误解，导致了重大争议。

- 福柯的作品内容丰富，观点独到，引发了大量学术争鸣和学术文章。近年来，因未在其研究的历史当中考虑殖民压迫和种族主义的作用，福柯的作品备受批评（"殖民主义"* 是指移居外国领土并剥削其人民的政策）。

其他思想

福柯在《性史（第一卷）：求知意志》中提出权力是分散的，这也是福柯在第一卷中最重要的次要观点。虽然他对权力的讨论可能看起来是次要的，仅仅是为了解释性分类本身的被建构本质，但事实上理解这一点对理解他整体作品的复杂观点至关重要。

这些观点占据了该书的核心地位，并在最后几章"性存在的部署"和"死亡的权利和管理生命的权力"中清晰呈现。福柯扩展了他对性存在的讨论，提出了一种新的权力理论，批评了认为权力是自上而下单向运作的观点。相反，他认为，权力是一种复杂的力量，能够实现欲望、满足快乐并且建构身份。

福柯关于权力分散的观点试图解释权力如何运作以及反抗如何

发生。这一命题对政治激进主义以及后马克思主义 *（指的是那些基于马克思主义理论，但在其基础上进行延伸、逆转或拓展的理论方法）和无政府主义政治理论 *（该理论秉持"等级制政府的制度是非法的"原则）中某些观点的发展具有很大影响。然而，福柯关于权力的论点同样也受到很多批评，引发了很多有益的讨论。

在书中最后一章"死亡的权利和管理生命的权力"中，福柯回顾了权力运作在早期社会与现代社会之间的差异。在早期社会，权力以"扣除"的方式运作；统治者通过征税，掠夺财富、土地、甚至生命来发挥其权威。在现代社会中，权力是"生产性的"，通过复杂的调节和控制来生产目标个体。比如剥夺或给予节育权，禁止或允许堕胎，支持异性恋，以及为每个家庭应该生育孩子的数量提供建议，这类举措都属于管理性行为和生殖行为的范畴。现代社会利用这些手段控制人口，确保公民遵循某种特定的生活方式。从这个意义上讲，现代社会将性视为一种可被管理的行为实践。

> "权力自下而来；也就是说，统治者和被统治者之间，在权力关系的根源上并不存在完全的对立，也不是一切对立的起源。"
>
> —— 米歇尔·福柯：《性史（第一卷）：求知意志》

思想探究

在《性史（第一卷）》中，福柯指出，我们思考自己和他人的性存在的方式与现代科学机构所给出的性别分类密切相关。科学界对我们如何看待人类行为、欲望以及我们自身有很大的影响。当科学家告诉我们什么东西不健康或不正常时，我们通常会相信他们。

如果我们不质疑这些想法，而是将它们视为事实，那我们就已在不知情的情况下陷入权力关系中。粗略地说，这就是等级体系下权力运作的方式。反抗权威的努力也不例外，因为反抗并不能从外部发生，因此反抗的前提是置身于权力关系中。

然而，这个重要的观点也导致了很多人的误解。人们经常误解福柯的论点，认为既然权力无处不在，无法摆脱，因此抵抗是徒劳的。[1] 事实上，福柯的观点恰恰相反。他论证的目的是挑战先前的观点，即认定我们需要反抗的权力是单一不变的。用他的话来说，"统治者和被统治者之间没有完全的对立。"[2] 而且，"有权力的地方，就会有抵抗产生，或者更确切地说，抵抗永远不会处于权力关系之外。"[3]

福柯想要阐述的是，任何形式的抵抗都必须首先承认它已经置身于权力关系之中。抵抗并不是徒劳的；问题的关键在于，抵抗者必须认识到他们并不是从摆脱权力约束的纯粹立场进行反抗的。美国酷儿研究学者大卫·哈尔珀林＊进一步解释了福柯所谈论的权力，他认为"福柯的一些左翼批评者可能单纯地误解了他'权力无处不在'的观点。所谓'权力无处不在'，福柯并不将权力视为强迫性的和不可抗拒的力量。相反，他指的是所谓的自由主义权力。这种权力认为自己的权力对象是'自由主体'，并完全通过与'自由主体'及其自由的关系来定义自身。"[4]

换句话说，制度通过规范人们如何谈论性以及社会如何定义"健康"或"不健康"的性行为或偏好来发挥其权威。但这些社会规范反过来又获得了自己的生命（姑且打个比喻），以统治者无法预见的方式塑造人们的观点和行为。权力和性存在在现代意义中是相互关联的，因为性存在同时受到直接（通过规章制度）管制和间接（通过无法溯源的社会规范）管制。

被忽视之处

《性史（第一卷）》引发了大量学术争鸣，随后有相当多的学术文章讨论了书中提出的各种观点。学者们质疑了其中一些观点，包括福柯论点中带有的欧洲中心主义＊色彩，即其论证很大程度上限于欧洲文化，而忽略了其他种族和民族（包括在福柯著书时，那些仍然生活在欧洲殖民统治下、或刚刚获得独立的民族）的性存在及相关观点。

1988年，在该书最初出版仅12年后，福柯的欧洲中心主义思想成为辩论的主题。在《文化的困境》（1988）一书中，美国人类学家詹姆斯·克利福德＊警告说，福柯的研究方法带有"肆无忌惮的种族中心主义"性质，而这"导致了对其他文化中类似问题的忽视"。[5] 类似的反对意见来自后殖民主义＊研究领域（探究殖民主义的各种文化和社会遗留问题）。例如，学者佳亚特里·斯皮瓦克＊在她著名的文章《底层人能说话吗？》中，将福柯置于西方文学传统之中审视，西方文学传统并不承认非西方人的观点和能动力（行动的力量）。

直到1995年，美国人类学家安·斯托勒＊的《种族和欲望教育：福柯的〈性史〉和殖民视角下的〈词与物〉》（1995）一书问世，才真正拉开了从后殖民主义角度对福柯进行丰富的讨论和颠覆性重读的序幕。斯托勒认为，福柯忽视了西方的现代性在很大程度上是通过与非欧洲人的相互作用而形成的，种族主义、殖民主义和奴隶制在其中发挥了重要作用。斯托勒虽然支持福柯的观点，但她认为，福柯所呈现的欧洲性史未能考虑到欧洲中产阶级身份是怎样在很大程度上相对于殖民地文化而塑造的。她质问道："为什么对福柯来说，殖民地人们的身体不能是 19 世纪欧洲性存在的表达场所？"[6]

基于欧洲殖民者与被殖民者（在非洲、亚洲和大洋洲）之间的不平等权力，通过重新思考性史，斯托勒一书揭示了福柯作品中被忽视的一面：资产阶级认识自我的方式和种族之间的关系。斯托勒的作品没有背弃福柯想要打破关于性身份刻板印象的总体目标，她为《性史（第一卷）》提供了一种富有成效的、具有文化特异性的批评方法，开辟了在殖民统治研究中运用福柯思想的新途径。[7]

1. 大卫·哈尔珀林：《圣福柯：走向同性恋运动》，纽约：牛津大学出版社，1995年，第 18 页。

2. 米歇尔·福柯：《性史（第一卷）：求知意志》，罗伯特·赫尔利译，伦敦：企鹅出版社，1998 年，第 94 页。

3. 福柯：《性史（第一卷）》，第 95 页。

4. 哈尔珀林：《圣福柯》，第 18 页。

5. 詹姆斯·克利福德：《文化的困境：20 世纪的民族志、文学和艺术》，马萨诸塞州坎布里奇：哈佛大学出版社，1988 年，第 264—265 页。

6. 安·劳拉·斯托勒：《种族和欲望教育：福柯的〈性史〉和殖民视角下的〈词与物〉》，北卡罗来纳州达勒姆：杜克大学出版社，1995 年，第 i 页。

7. 斯托勒：《种族和欲望教育》，第 1—2 页。

7 历史成就

要点 ⚷━┅

- 福柯独到的分析方法引入了一种新的思考方式,来思考性存在、知识的生产和权力的运作,从而影响了人文社科内的多个领域。

- 1976 年《性史(第一卷)》正式出版,1978 年英文译本出版,对同性恋和酷儿活动家产生了巨大影响。他们希望挑战被广泛接受的关于性存在和性别身份的假设,目的是重塑权力结构和平等的天平。

- 虽然福柯的著作被公认为是一部开创性的作品,但也受到女权主义者和后殖民主义学者的批评,他们认为福柯的作品带有男性中心主义*(专注于男性经历)和欧洲中心主义色彩。

观点评价

福柯的《性史(第一卷):求知意志》在反对弗洛伊德—马克思主义对性存在的分析方面具有高度的原创性。弗洛伊德—马克思主义性观点当时在知识界占主导地位。福柯认为性是一系列由社会建构并由科学机构塑造的想法,这些想法被用来规范个人和群体。福柯通过复杂的历史分析和理论分析来论证这一论点,该分析追溯了 17 世纪末一种将性作为科学研究对象的新学科的兴起过程。正是这类学科的兴起所带来的新方法给后来将人们标记为正常或异常的做法提供了依据。

福柯的方法催生了一整套关于性存在的研究。这些研究在 20世纪 90 年代大幅扩展,如今在学术辩论中占据主导地位。这类研究将性存在视为权力的产物，而不是权力的严格对立面。

性存在被视为权力的产物这一观点与福柯另一个独到的观点相关，即福柯对权力的理解。他提出了一个重要的主张，即权力不仅仅是以消极否定的方式运作，比如，它并不仅仅是为了禁止或抑制那些希望得到畅快表达的本能欲望（例如"性冲动"）。权力也不仅仅是在一个简单的自上而下的方向上运作。对于福柯而言，权力也是富有生产性的，因为权力创造了偏好、取向和欲望。

这种观念认为权力不是一种无所不能的力量，而是一系列关系，这被证明是后马克思主义政治理论发展的关键。福柯的作品一直被后马克思主义者视为核心作品。后马克思主义的代表学者包括阿根廷政治理论家埃内斯托·拉克劳 *、比利时政治理论家尚泰尔·慕非 * 和意大利哲学家安东尼奥·内格里 *。

> "快乐和权力不会消灭或反对彼此。他们寻求彼此、互相重叠，并相互加强。它们通过刺激和兴奋组成的复杂机制联系在一起。"
>
> —— 米歇尔·福柯：《性史（第一卷）：求知意志》

当时的成就

虽然福柯作品的标题表明它研究的是性存在的历史，但将其视为传统意义上的历史文本就过于简单化了。福柯从没想过自己是一位专业的历史学家；他试图揭示人们对现代西方社会所秉持的基本假设。他的作品还考察了与性实践的表现和理解方式相关的真相、知识和权力等概念。

通过挑战这些立场，福柯的作品让我们以新的方式思考性存在。福柯将性存在视为社会条件的产物，而不是纯粹的本能。此外，福柯将"权力"视为关系和社会力量的多重作用，而不仅仅是统治者使用或威胁使用武力。这个论点在知识界中产生了长久的影响。

福柯的《性史（第一卷）》在学术界之外也是具有开创性意义的。1976 年首次出版，两年后英文版面世，该书在 20 世纪 80 年代和 90 年代对同性恋和酷儿活动家产生了重大影响。因对酷儿理论的发展做出杰出贡献而闻名的学者大卫·哈尔珀林教授曾说，当 20 世纪 80 年代后期纽约的同性恋活动家被问及他们所受的影响来自何处时，他们会"毫不犹豫而且无一例外地回答是福柯的《性史（第一卷）》"。[1]

局限性

尽管福柯提出的说法确实具有开创性，但由于该书篇幅较短，因此所提论点没有能够得到深入分析。从这个意义上讲，整个文本似乎是对接下来更多内容的美好展望。《性史（第一卷）：求知意志》本打算作为六卷本中的第一卷，因此不难理解其作为开卷的作用。同样值得一提的是，该文本并不像真正的历史研究那样全面、严谨，所以这一点颇受诟病。[2]

该书最常被提及的局限之一是，它几乎完全只关注性存在在西方现代性中所扮演的角色。然而，有人可能会反驳这种说法，认为福柯研究的对象——"现代性"——不仅仅指的是西方世界的一段历史时期，同时也是指一系列实践、求知的方法以及传播到世界各地的行为规则。以科学知识为基础的对性存在的讨论就是一个例子，这些科学知识（现在或过去）将某些行为定义为"变态"

或"病态",而这样的讨论现在已扩展到世界其他地区。换句话说，《性史（第一卷）：求知意志》得出的结论同样适用于分析欧洲之外的社会和人群。

其他对原著的批评更不容忽视。例如，福柯仅在第三部分"性科学"中提及了当前或古代欧洲以外的文明中的性存在。在这一部分中，他对比分析了所谓的"产生性真相的两个伟大过程"。[3] 福柯认为在中国、日本、印度、罗马和阿拉伯—穆斯林国家，人们通过色情作品*来理解关于性的真相，也就是说通过愉悦和经验本身来掌握。这与现代西方社会形成鲜明对比。在现代西方社会中，关于性的真相是通过性科学来展现的。这是一种基于知识生产来理解性存在的手段，例如科学研究或忏悔仪式。这一分析引发了突尼斯社会学家法蒂·特里基*等学者的批评，他们认为这种观点幼稚且不可靠。[4]

对于《性史（第一卷）》，女性主义批评者也批评其"对性暴力的盲目性"[5]及其男性中心主义色彩——即仅关注男性经历。[6]书中最常被谴责的部分是福柯对1867年发生的一个案件的描述。案件描述的是一位来自法国拉普科特镇的农民因"从一个小女孩那里得到一些爱抚"而被押送到警局。[7]令福柯觉得不可思议的是，这个农民因为自己的行为而变成了"司法判决、医疗干预、临床检查以及一整套理论阐述"的对象。[8]福柯认为，个人变成"医学和知识的纯粹对象"[9]的方式，表明性行为在现代如何通过法律—精神病学所给出的分类来揭示个体的内在自我（在本案中，犯人是一个具备性骚扰或强奸动机的人）。女权主义作家批评这种解释，是因为福柯忽视受害者和她所遭受的暴力，只从男性犯人的角度看待问题。[10]

1. 参见大卫·哈尔珀林:《圣福柯:走向同性恋运动》,纽约:牛津大学出版社,1995 年,第 16 页。

2. 参见杰瑞米·R.卡雷特:《福柯与宗教:精神肉体和政治灵性》,伦敦:劳特利奇出版社,2000 年,第 131 页;伊丽莎白·A.克拉克:"福柯,父和性",《美国宗教学会杂志》第 56 卷,1988 年第 4 期,第 625 页。

3. 米歇尔·福柯:《性史(第一卷):求知意志》,罗伯特·赫尔利译,伦敦:企鹅出版社,1998 年,第 57 页。

4. 珍妮特·阿法瑞和凯文·B.安德森:"地中海地区和穆斯林社会中的福柯、性别与男同性恋研究",载《福柯与伊朗革命:性别与伊斯兰主义的诱惑力》,芝加哥:芝加哥大学出版社,2005 年,第 138—162 页,引用摘于 141 页。

5. 凯莉·H.鲍尔:"差不多被性侵:福柯,因果关系,以及女权主义者对性暴力的批判",《哲学》第 3 卷,2013 年,第 1 期,第 53 页。

6. 凯特·索珀:"生产力矛盾",载《反对福柯:福柯与女权主义之间的紧张关系》,卡罗琳·拉马扎诺格鲁编,纽约:劳特利奇出版社,1993 年,第 29 页。

7. 福柯:《性史(第一卷)》,第 31 页。

8. 福柯:《性史(第一卷)》,第 31 页。

9. 福柯:《性史(第一卷)》,第 31 页。

10. 详情参见鲍尔:"差不多被性侵"。

8 著作地位

要点 🔑

- 1976 年出版的《性史（第一卷）》是福柯生前最后的作品之一，标志着他思想演变的重要时刻。

- 与福柯的其他著作一样，《性史（第一卷）》关注权力和知识，以及身份的构建，但它的分析方法却很新颖。它通过"治理术"*的概念（旨在塑造公民行为而非公开压制的治理方法）和"生命权力"*（福柯用这个词来形容控制个体和整个人口的技术"爆炸"）来分析这些问题。

- 福柯对酷儿理论以及性别和性存在研究领域的影响无可争议。《规训和惩罚》以及《性史》三卷本是福柯最知名、引用频率最高的书籍。

定位

米歇尔·福柯的《性史（第一卷）：求知意志》探究性存在主题。关于他对权力运作的看法可以追溯到其早期的著作，其中最突出的是《规训与惩罚》。该书涉及监狱运作，在《性史》出版的前一年，即 1975 年出版。福柯认为《性史》是其早期作品的延续。[1]

在《规训与惩罚》中，福柯讨论了 18 和 19 世纪西方刑罚制度（特别是监狱体制）的变化。他富有说服力地指出，当时对犯罪者的身体虐待逐渐让位于基于犯罪分析的惩罚，这些分析试图找出罪犯犯罪的原因，并将科学研究推进到所谓的"犯罪心理"研究。这些研究还用来确定罪犯是否可以改过自新，变得"正常"，并重新融入社会。与其将罪犯判处死刑，不如由医生来设法根除其不良行为。在此期间，"一系列知识、技术、'科学'话语的论述形成，并与惩罚的权力实践交错在一起。"[2] 在《性史（第一卷）》里可以很明显地找到这些论点的痕迹，该卷也涉及知识如何用于催生新形式的监管和控制。

根据艾伦·D. 斯克里夫特*等学者的观点，福柯的写作生涯可以分为三个不同的时期：早期的"考古"阶段，在此期间他专注于话语和语言问题（"考古学"是通过研究人类活动遗骸和分析文物来研究历史）；第二个是"谱系"阶段，关注权力与知识之间的关系；第三个是涉及主体性*（这里指的是个人自我或身份发展的方式）的"道德"阶段。

对斯克里夫特来说，福柯"考古"时期的作品包括《疯癫与文明》（1964）、《词与物》（1966）和《知识考古学》*（1969），它们共同关注"知识、语言、和真理的关系"。在"谱系"时期，福柯特别关注权力，其作品包括《规训与惩罚》（1975）和《性史（第一卷）》（1976）。"道德"时期的作品包括《性史（第二卷）》和《性史（第三卷）》（1984）。这个时期的作品与福柯以前的作品大不相同，专注于"道德/性主体或自我的构建"。[3] 然而，这并不是唯一的归类方式，而且也有人认为这种方式过于简单化。福柯本人可能会拒绝这样的标签，因为他对固定类别持怀疑态度，并且他对创造这些固定类别的学者的动机抱有极高的探究热忱。

> "权力无处不在：这不是因为它有着把一切都整合到自己万能的统一体之中的特权，而是因为它在每一时刻、在一切地点或者在不同地点的相互关系之中都会生产出来。权力到处都有，这不是说它囊括一切，而是指它来自各处。"
>
> —— 米歇尔·福柯：《性史（第一卷）：求知意志》

整合

福柯在书中以一个复杂的论述引出了他重要的思想观点。他在《性史（第一卷）》中间部分的地方提出了关于权力在现代社会中的运作方式的议题。

根据福柯的论述，权力——特别是现代权力——并不是从上到下地运作，毕竟"统治者和被统治者之间并没有完全的对立"。[4] 因此，并不存在单一的极权式的"权力"来抑制和禁绝欲望：权力关系是的的确确存在的，它通过不同的手段获得协助和加强，这些手段旨在控制，正如福柯所描述的那样，"人的存在，把人作为活体来控制。"[5]

福柯引入了"生命权力"一词来指代这一观点，这是他后期作品中最重要的概念之一。生命权力还与福柯的另一个概念"治理术"尤其相关。他创造了这个术语来定义旨在塑造公民行为（行为和思想）而不是进行公开压制的治理实践，例如，利用有关性的科学知识来对性加以规范。

尽管福柯的不同著作论述了许多共同的主题，但它们也表达了相当明显的差异，这些差异同时也反映了他思想的演变。例如，福柯的早期作品，如《疯癫与文明》和《临床医学的诞生》（1963），受到结构主义思想的影响，与后来的作品形成鲜明对比，后来的作品可划入后结构主义范畴。

作为一种理论方法，结构主义企图探索使文化具备意义的元素，认为研究这些元素与其所属的深层结构和体系的关系能更好地理解这些元素。后结构主义则质疑这些结构的存在，不赞同"人们可以完全确定客观知识存在"的观点，因为任何分析都从文化预设开始，人们也无法跳出这一预设进行思考分析。

在《知识考古学》中，福柯将他的早期作品描述为"非常不完美的草图"，[6]认为那些作品"令他感到惭愧……因为分析是将文化作为整体来进行的。"[7]这句话不仅说明福柯早期和晚期作品之间存在差异，还显示了结构主义和后结构主义之间的区别。

结构主义思想试图通过社会的结构来理解文化的某个特定元素。因此，例如在《临床医学的诞生》一书中，福柯通过考察临床医学的历史追踪整个医学专业的发展，以思考他所谓的"医学凝视"[*]如何生产有关人体和人类健康的知识。相比之下，后结构主义者不会声称能够完全客观地理解这一主题，而是承认，作为研究的参与者，他或她总会带有主观偏见。换句话说，在福柯后来的著作中，他意识到自己同样是在一个体制内进行写作。作为 20 世纪法国的教授，他能理解的范围也受到限制。

意义

虽然自从原著出版以来，关于性存在的学术讨论已经发生了很大变化，但《性史（第一卷）》仍然是酷儿理论、性别和性存在研究领域的重要文献，也是被引用次数最多的文本之一。酷儿理论是一种文化分析方法，从承认性别认同和知识本身的不稳定性和不确定性这一基础展开。性存在研究是对性存在（我们的性偏好和性取向）的构建和理解方式的探究。

《性史（第一卷）》自首次出版以来，福柯在书中提出的理论经常被世界各地备受尊敬的学者引用并作为参考。据《泰晤士高等教育》杂志报道，福柯是 2007 年人文社科领域被引用次数最多的作者。[8]

　　《性史（第一卷）》可以被看作对福柯早期思想进行融合与拓展的结晶。该书发展并充分地表达了权力、知识和身体之间的关系，这一关系对福柯所有的著作都有至关重要的意义。如果要概括福柯学术生涯的目标，那么它可能是：理解权力如何在社会和学术领域中运作，理解权力与知识之间的关系，以及理解长久以来人体、人类性存在和诸如疯癫、犯罪和监视等概念是如何被用来观察或改变公民的行为。《性史（第一卷）》是福柯向他的学术目标迈出的重要一步。

1. 戴维·马塞：《米歇尔·福柯的生平》，纽约：万神殿出版社，1993 年，第 354 页。
2. 米歇尔·福柯：《规训与惩罚》，阿兰·谢里登译，纽约：兰登书屋，1977 年，第 23 页。
3. 艾伦·D. 斯克里夫特：《尼采的法国遗产：后结构主义的谱系》，伦敦：劳特利奇出版社，1995 年，第 35—37 页。
4. 米歇尔·福柯：《性史（第一卷）：求知意志》，罗伯特·赫尔利译，伦敦：企鹅出版社，1998 年，第 98 页。
5. 福柯：《性史（第一卷）》，第 89 页。
6. 米歇尔·福柯：《知识考古学》，阿兰·谢里登译，伦敦：塔维斯托克出版社，1972 年，第 15 页。
7. 福柯：《知识考古学》，第 15 页。
8. "2007 年人文学科被引用最多的作者"，《泰晤士高等教育》，登录日期 2015 年 11 月 15 日，http://www.timeshighereducation.co.uk/405956.article。

第三部分：学术影响

9 最初反响

要点 🗝

- 《性史（第一卷）》出版时受到了许多学者的反对。女权主义批评家对该书的讨论尤为热烈，其中部分批评家支持米歇尔·福柯对性分类的质疑，而另一部分批评家则批评他对性暴力的一些看法。

- 虽然福柯在采访中针对一些批评做出了回应，但他并未参与大多数讨论。

- 然而，在其后出版的《性史》第二卷和第三卷中，侧重点发生改变，表明福柯似乎在尝试接受批评者的意见。

批评

米歇尔·福柯的这部《性史（第一卷）：求知意志》在首次出版时饱受争议。[1] 出版后的头几年，主要的批评并非针对整部作品，而是作品的某些方面。虽然许多批评基于马克思主义和精神分析的观点，但对于《性史（第一卷）》最持久也最有成效的早期辩论来自女权主义领域。

1982 年，美国学者兼作家毕蒂·马丁*曾提醒读者："福柯挑战传统分类的危险在于，如果要给一个'合乎逻辑的'结论的话……会使女性受压迫的问题显得过时。"[2] 她还提醒女权主义者"不要被福柯的作品诱导"。[3] 尽管女权主义者总体上支持福柯的方法论以及他对性分类构建本质的论述，但像马丁这样的学者仍然指出了福柯作品在解决两性平等的社会需求方面的局限性。

其他女权主义者批评了福柯关于性暴力的论述。第一篇谈及该问题的文章是法国女权主义学者和活动家莫妮克·普拉扎*的《我们的代价与他们的利益》（1978）。该文批评了福柯在1977年发表的有关法国强奸罪法案的观点。福柯的这个观点是在《性史（第一卷）》出版一年后在一次关于修改法案的讨论中提出的。福柯拓展了在《性史（第一卷）》中的某些看法，称强奸案件应像所有其他"暴力行为"（比如殴打）一样受到法律制裁，[4]而施暴者的"性存在"不应受到法律的惩罚。

普拉扎在文章中试图拆解福柯的论点，并谴责他事实上"去除强奸中的性成分"。她称福柯将性存在视为权力部署（使用）的产物，其中最大的受害者是女性的身体。普拉扎称，"因为福柯默许以特权占有女性身体为目标的权力部署"[5]（或者说，默许以强迫行为控制女性身体），福柯其实创造了一个与他一直反对的权力结构相同的结构（即男性长久以来占有女性身体的方式）。正如两位英国评论家所写的那样，"在试图以惩罚性暴力但将其中的性存在合法化的方式来重写强奸法案的同时，他正在捍卫男性拥有女性身体的既有权利。"[6]

> "重要的是，性不仅是有关感觉和愉悦、法律和禁忌的问题，同样也是有关真实和谬误的问题，性的'真实性'变成了根本的、有用的、危险的、重要的或令人敬畏的问题。简单地说，性成了'真实性'问题。"
>
> —— 米歇尔·福柯：《性史（第一卷）：求知意志》

回应

福柯于1984年离世，这是《性史（第一卷）》出版后的第八年、英译本出版后的第六年，而大多数关于福柯作品的学术批评是在 20 世纪 80 年代和 90 年代出现的，因此他没有机会对这些批评作出回应。

不过，起初的评论还是得到了他本人的回应。在《性史（第一卷）》出版几年后的一次采访中，福柯便回应了女权主义者的批评。女权主义认为他忽略性暴力并去除了强奸中的性成分。[7] 他说："我主张的是'性选择自由'而非'性行为自由'，因为强奸等强迫发生的性行为是绝不被允许的。"[8]

对福柯最常见的批评之一认为，既然福柯指出权力并非完全局限于政府和国家，而是通过整个社会起作用的，那么抵抗是不可能的。然而在后来一次采访中，他直接对这一批评进行了反驳："有种观点认为'权力遍布各处，自由没有空间'，这在我看来是非常不准确的。认为权力是控制一切、不允许自由空间的统治体系，这样的想法并不是出自我的作品。"[9]

冲突与共识

福柯也认识到自己的作品需要修改。尽管他的作品中有许多相同的主题，但他早期研究和后期研究之间的明显差异，表明他为了发展和完善思想而作出了巨大努力。

也有证据表明，他的方法论及分析角度的部分变化是缘于其他学者对他早期作品的批评。例如，在《性史》第二卷和第三卷中福柯谈到对一些社会权力系统的抵制实践，这可能是对早期批评的回应，为了解决第一卷中未解决的问题。虽然福柯从未对此做出正面回应，但是和第一卷相比，后两卷的语气明显转变，很有可能是受到了其他学者对第一卷作出的批评的影响。这种转变也促使女权主义批评家对福柯在第三卷中"关心自我"部分的内容给予了更多的赞同。对于很多人来说，这部作品对性别身份的本质和如何理解性行为的讨论都具有道德层面的深层意义。这本书提供了一种在个体对他者责任基础上理解个体身份的模式。[10]

最后值得一提的是，尽管福柯的《性史（第一卷）》一开始受到了许多负面评价，但是它带来了对性存在、欲望和制度权力之间如何相互关联的全新理解。尽管他对强奸等具体问题的一些看法仍然存在争议，但关于知识、权力和身份之间关系的论述仍然具有很大影响。福柯在人文社科领域仍然是被引用次数最多的作家之一，也是自 20 世纪 70 年代以来最具影响力的学者之一。

1. 丹尼尔·德费尔："年代学"，《福柯研究指南》，克里斯托弗·法尔宗等编，奇切斯特：威利父子出版社，2013 年，第 63 页。

2. 毕蒂·马丁："女权主义、批判与福柯"，《新德国批判》第 27 卷，1982 年，第 17 页。

3. 马丁："女权主义、批判与福柯"，第 7 页。

4. 米歇尔·福柯："疯癫圈"，《法国女权主义理论：导论》，丹尼·卡瓦拉罗著，伦敦：绵延出版社，2003 年，第 102 页。

5. 莫妮克·普拉扎："我们的代价与他们的利益"，《性的问题：法国唯物主义女性主义》，戴安娜·伦纳德和丽莎·阿德金斯编，伦敦：泰勒和弗朗西斯出版社，1996 年，第 185 页。

6. 参见戴安娜·伦纳德和丽莎·阿德金斯："法国女权主义的重建：商品化、唯物主义和性"，《性的问题》，第 18 页。

7. 参见莫妮克·普拉扎："我们的代价与他们的利益"，《性的问题》，第 185 页。

8. 米歇尔·福柯："性选择，性行为"，詹姆斯·奥希金斯译，《米歇尔·福柯：

伦理学、主体性和真理》，保罗·拉比诺编，纽约：新新出版社，1997年，第143页。

9. 米歇尔·福柯："自我关怀的伦理作为一种自由的实践"，P. 阿拉纳弗和 D. 麦格劳斯译，《米歇尔·福柯：伦理学、主体性和真理》，保罗·拉比诺编，纽约：新新出版社，1997年，第293页。

10. 参见拉德尔·麦克沃特：《身体与愉悦：福柯与性规范化政治》，布卢明顿：印第安纳大学出版社，1999年，第196页；艾米·艾伦："福柯、女权主义与自我：自我变革的政治"，《女权主义与最后的福柯》，戴安娜·泰勒和凯伦·维茨编，芝加哥：伊利诺伊大学出版社，2004年，第235—257页。

10 后续争议

要点 🔑

- 福柯的《性史（第一卷）》改变了学术界对性存在的思考方式，影响了一些学术新领域的发展，包括酷儿理论和性别及性存在研究。

- 然而，福柯关于权力的观点与某些思想流派并不一致，这些思想流派主要包括正统的马克思主义、精神分析以及女权主义批评的一些分支，他们均建立在权力集中思想的基础上。

- 近年，福柯的生命权力和治理术理论激发了治理学研究*的发展。治理学研究借用他的思想方法来研究自由社会的治理方法。

应用与问题

《性史（第一卷）：求知意志》是米歇尔·福柯被引用次数最多、最具影响力的著作之一。这部作品对于很多重要思想家的作品乃至很多思想流派都产生了相当大的影响。与这部作品关系密切的学者众多，研究范围涵盖文化研究*（提出从人类学角度解读社会关系的学科）、哲学、文学和人类学等诸多领域。

然而，福柯在《性史（第一卷）》中论述权力分散的观点，与某些学派背道而驰。这一观点与诸如女权主义、正统马克思主义和精神分析等以权力集中概念为基础的学科观念相左。女权主义者认为权力与男性支配地位及社会的父权制*（男性统治）观念相关。而对于正统马克思主义者而言，权力集中在拥有金钱和社会地位的人手中。对于精神分析学家来说，权力在诸如父亲法则*（法国精神分析学家雅克·拉康*用来描述禁止乱伦等禁忌行为的法则）等概念中得以体现。这里提到的三种观点都与福柯的观点相矛盾。

特别是女权主义批评者，他们关注的对象最接近于《性史（第一卷）》的主题。这些批评者反复重申福柯的思想观念并不适合表达对父权制度及男性统治的抵制。此外，他们指出福柯对强奸和性暴力等话题所持有的立场并不清晰。

> "至少在弗洛伊德之前，不管是学者或理论家，关于性的话题，都对谈论的主题有所顾忌。似乎，所有论述，所有费力的预防和解析，不过是庞杂的步骤，意图只是为了逃避让人无法忍受的、充满危险的、关于性的真相。"
>
> —— 米歇尔·福柯:《性史（第一卷）: 求知意志》

思想流派

《性史（第一卷）》不隶属于任何学科门类。这部作品广泛推动了人文社科领域内的学术探讨，并改变了关于性存在、权力和知识的学术研究的演进历程。

酷儿理论、性别和性存在研究的学者们提炼福柯的观点，对男性/女性、同性恋/异性恋的分类标准提出了质疑。他们将性存在视为"历史性的独特经历"——即会随着历史环境而变化。[1] 正如文化历史学家塔姆辛·斯帕戈*在《福柯与酷儿理论》中所论证的，对于酷儿理论来说，福柯"可被视为催化剂（和）出发点"，"福柯为酷儿理论树立了很好的榜样，提供了理论前提，为新思想的诞生带来了源源不断的鞭策和动力。"[2] 美国酷儿研究学者大卫·哈尔珀林也指出，自从 1978 年英译《性史（第一卷）》出版以来，性学研究领域的进展"一直很快速，学术活动也十分频繁"。[3]

尤有价值的是福柯对于身体的关注，因为他不再将个体理解为具有不变身份的固定存在，这对进一步的研究帮助极大。那些试图构建性压迫和性别压迫理论的学者们，不用再接受"性别和性差异是固定的、自然的身份特征"这样的观点。

福柯的理论对于思想家有很高的价值，这些思想家包括《性别麻烦》（1990）的作者、美国性别研究学者朱迪斯·巴特勒＊和《暗柜认识论＊》（1990）的作者伊芙·塞奇威克。这里提到的两部作品是第一批将福柯思想扩散到大学人文系的著作，在美国学术界更是如此。两部作品延续了福柯的理论方法，试图挑战对于性分类的普遍理解（巴特勒探讨的是男／女的分类，塞奇威克则讨论同性恋／异性恋的分类）。也正是因为这两本书，福柯被誉为酷儿理论以及性别和性存在研究之父。

大卫·哈尔珀林为在学术界推广福柯的思想也出了一份力。他的作品中，有一部题为《同性恋一百年和其他关于希腊爱情的论文》（1990）的著作，是受到福柯启发后，以新的理论框架来研究古希腊男性之间的性行为和价值观，并将其与资产阶级社会（即现代西方社会）形成对比。凭借这本书与他写的福柯传记《圣福柯：走向同性恋运动》（1995），哈尔珀林为福柯思想在人文学科的传播做出了贡献。

当代研究

福柯在《性史（第一卷）》中提出的观点，影响范围已超出了性存在研究的学术争鸣。20 世纪 90 年代伊始，福柯的思想就被应用于人文社科领域。最近，又被应用在关于治理学的探讨中。

尤其值得关注的是福柯对治理学研究的影响。该术语源自福柯的治理术概念，这是他在生命最后几年中发展的理念，用来描述权力（"治理"）塑造主体或个人的方式，包括如何塑造思想和信念（"心态"）。虽然福柯在《性史（第一卷）》出版几年后才创造这一术语，但是在该书中福柯就已经提到并发展了"治理"概念所仰赖的"权力分散"思想。福柯将这种分散的权力称为"生命权力"——这种权力产生于非平等（不平等）、非固定的（易变）关系网络上无数相互作用的节点，并且试图管理、调控生命。[4]

治理学研究基于许多理论学家（包括英国著名的社会学家尼克拉斯·罗斯*）的观点，并直接引用了福柯的思想观念。该研究关注自由社会中治理的运作方式（这里的"自由"指的是其经济意义上的含义，用于描述资本主义制度的社会性后果）。根据这个流派的观点，自由社会的权力不仅仅是压制性和禁止性的，而且还分布在各种机制、制度之间，并通过治理术来塑造人们的行为模式。此想法来自福柯对知识生产的理解，同时福柯的另一个观点——将性作为科学课题并利用研究结果，对病态（疾病）和变态进行区别，最终为国家提供了控制公民的新方式——也对治理思想影响很大。

随后，这些领域关于治理的学术写作在 21 世纪之初让人们重新开始讨论权力与经济之间的关系，尤其是新自由主义*经济学说。[5]根据新自由主义，无论社会后果如何，政府都应避免干预市场和国民经济的运作。

1. 参见米歇尔·福柯：《性史（第二卷）：快感的享用》，罗伯特·赫尔利译，纽约：兰登书屋，2012 年，第 4 页。

2. 塔姆辛·斯帕戈：《福柯与酷儿理论》，剑桥：图标出版社，1999 年，第 17 页；大卫·哈尔珀林，纽约：牛津大学出版社，1995 年，第 10 页。

3. 大卫·哈尔珀林：《同性恋一百年和其他关于希腊爱情的论文》，伦敦：劳特利奇出版社，1990 年，第 34 页。

4. 米歇尔·福柯：《性史（第一卷）：求知意志》，罗伯特·赫尔利译，伦敦：企鹅出版社，1998 年，第 94 页。

5. 参见温迪·拉内尔："新自由主义：政策、意识形态和治理"，《政治经济研究》第 63 卷，2000 年，第 5—25 页；南茜·弗雷泽："从纪律到灵活化？在全球化阴影下重读福柯"，《星丛》第 10 卷 2003 年第 2 期，第 160—171 页。

11 当代印迹

要点 ⚷

- 福柯的《性史（第一卷）》备受推崇，被广泛引用，直接影响了有关性存在的学术辩论，间接影响了公众对性别和性取向的理解。
- 福柯的作品常被看作后结构主义思想的典范，因为它对普世真理持怀疑态度；然而，这也使之与自由主义背道而驰。
- 围绕福柯关于性存在的一些观点、男人／女人或异性恋／同性恋的二元分类模型和有关知识建构的本质所产生的争议，也让他的作品成为人们津津乐道的话题。

地位

米歇尔·福柯的《性史（第一卷）：求知意志》被视为人文社科领域的开创性文本。这部作品被广泛引用，其主要和次要思想理论在法语和英语学术界的各个学科都有广泛应用。例如，分别于 1990 年和 1998 年成立的学术期刊《性史期刊》和《性存在》都在很大程度上受到了福柯的研究方法、研究范围和分析方法的影响。此外，福柯的想法决定了性存在话题在男同性恋、女同性恋、女权主义者社群中的讨论方向，以及相关运动的话语和实践。酷儿研究者大卫·哈尔珀林进一步指出，20 世纪 80 年代与艾滋病有关的政治运动从《性史（第一卷）》中获得很大启发。[1]

福柯在《性史（第一卷）》中的论述在公众中并不广为人知，但对于那些熟悉他思想的人来说，他对于当今有关性少数群体辩论的影响是毋庸置疑的。特别是福柯的"性存在是社会和历史环境的产物，而不仅仅是生物学决定的"这一论点，极大地（尽管是间接地）影响了关于性别认同*和性取向的普遍争论。此外，另一观点也与福柯紧密相关：上层机构利用性存在来控制群众，增加繁殖需要（例如，通过宣传生育和核心家庭的概念）。这在当代艺术中具有很大的影响力，例如，纽约艺术家大卫·沃纳洛维奇*的作品中就有很好的体现。[2]

大卫·沃纳洛维奇是20世纪80年代、90年代著名的艾滋病活动家。在记录他这段时期积极活动的回忆录中，沃纳洛维奇详细地叙述了自己对那些被称为"风险"群体的艾滋病受害者，尤其是男同性恋患者被刻意边缘化和污名化的反感。基于福柯所述的以性存在来对人们作出"不道德"或"患病"诊断的观点，他论证了政治家如何利用艾滋病来为"妖魔化"同性恋者的种种行径开脱。

福柯的作品本身也是艺术创作的主题，例如1993年英国广播公司的纪录片《米歇尔·福柯：超越善与恶》，[3] 展示了福柯生平和作品的影像。由瑞士艺术家托马斯·赫希霍恩*搭建的"福柯24小时"艺术装置也备受好评。[4]

此书的重要性超越了其主题本身。福柯在《性史（第一卷）》中最后两部分中提出的论点尤其如此：在第四部分"性存在的部署"和第五部分"死亡的权利和管理生命的权力"中，他分析了现代社会的权力观念。这影响了医药科学（如临床精神病学）就医疗保健与社会控制系统之间如何关联的思考。[5]

> "我们必须……抛开'现代工业社会将进入愈发升级的性压抑时代'这一假设。我们不仅目睹了非传统性行为的爆发，而且，更重要的是，一种与传统法律大不相同的部署，哪怕在部分地区被依令禁止，但还是带来了……各种快乐的激增和性存在的极大丰富。有人说……权力机构已经小心谨慎，假装不知道他们禁止了什么……但是……他们完全清楚……而且已经变得十分明显了。"
>
> ——米歇尔·福柯：《性史（第一卷）：求知意志》

互动

自由主义是对福柯的作品最抱怀疑态度的思想流派之一。社会自由主义者关心公民权利、民主和社会平等的进步。自由主义重视诸如理性、选择、自治（不受胁迫地行事）和平等权利等因素。比如，自由女权主义*者坚持认为，女性和男性应该在社会中享有同等机会，促进对女性的社会包容性（包括在工作场所）将有助于性别平等。这种观点建立在某些普世真理之上，例如男女平等、人人平等。但这一观点与后结构主义（包括福柯的分析方法——《性史（第一卷）》常被认为是后结构主义的典型作品）不相容，后者对普世的人文主义价值观持怀疑态度，并认为所有所谓"真理"实际上取决于其他因素。

出于同样的原因，自由女权主义者常常批评福柯和他的追随者，因为他们的理论方法没有任何支持女性、反对性别不平等和父权制的观点。福柯称，我们理解性别分类的方式是来源于社会建构，而不是源于两性之间的生理上的差异。这样的想法挑战了自由主义认为"男性和女性是两种自然分割、对立的性别"的观点。

自由女权主义者也批评福柯的反本质主义*思想（福柯认为事

物并不存在真正深刻的差异，比如男／女或异性恋／同性恋）。1999年，美国法律和哲学教授玛莎·努斯鲍姆*在一篇题为《模仿专家：朱迪斯·巴特勒的臀部失败主义》的文章中强烈抨击了女权主义者追随福柯的思想倾向。努斯鲍姆对女权主义理论家朱迪斯·巴特勒提出批评："看来，太多年轻学者想定义当代的女权主义。"[6]她还因为福柯没有提出如何抵抗压迫的看法而进行抨击。努斯鲍姆认为，福柯对性的分析方法缺乏"社会公正和人类尊严的规范理论"，[7]这导致了"鸦雀无声（平静接受）和望而却步"。[8]

持续争议

对于那些以"生物决定论"来解释性行为的传统理论来说，福柯的理论是一种持续挑战。更确切地说，《性史（第一卷）》直接对抗实证主义*学科，如生物学或生物人类学*（"实证主义"在这里指的是支持"知识来源于观察"的观点；"生物人类学"是从人类有机体的长久历史和有机体本性来研究人类行为的研究领域）。这两门学科都将性取向、偏好和品味视为生物进化因素。而那些受到福柯作品启发的人，就会质疑自然或真实人类本性的存在。像福柯一样，这些追随者更愿意谈论有关性的某些知识是如何产生的，以及这些知识如何反过来影响我们的性欲以及性的实践和认知方式。

关于上述内容，我们可以判断，福柯从根本上挑战了自由主义思想流派，具体而言就是自由主义对性存在的分析方式。在不否认政治行动或抵制压迫的必要性的前提下，福柯的作品有助于对抗本质主义*（认为存在人性本质）以呼吁人权。[9]这些质疑符合福柯的论述精神，他倾向于将那些被视为理所当然的观念置于历史背景中考察并提出质疑。

1. 参见安·劳拉·斯托勒:《种族与欲望教育:福柯的〈性史〉和殖民视角下的〈词与物〉》,北卡罗来纳州达勒姆:杜克大学出版社,1995年,第1—2页。

2. 参见托马斯·罗奇:"感知和性:福柯、沃纳洛维奇和生命权力",《星云:多学科学术期刊》第6卷,2009年第3期,第155—173页。

3. 《米歇尔·福柯:超越善与恶》,英国电影协会,1993年,登录日期2016年3月6日,http://www.bfi.org.uk/films-tv-people/4ce2b7c9bb0c5。

4. 托马斯·赫希霍恩:"福柯24小时",2004年10月1日,登录日期2016年3月6日,http://1995-2015.undo.net/it/mostra/21388。

5. 参见罗宾·班顿和艾伦·彼得森编:《福柯、健康与医学》,伦敦:劳特利奇出版社,2002年;詹尼弗·拉登:《精神病学哲学:指南》,牛津:牛津大学出版社,2004年,第248—249页;安·布莱纳曼:"当代社会理论与心理健康社会学研究",《心理健康,社会镜像》,威廉·R.阿维森编,纽约:斯普林格出版社,2007年出版,第95—126页;安·罗杰斯和大卫·皮尔格林:《心理健康与疾病社会学》,梅登黑德:开放大学出版社,2014年,第37—52页。

6. 玛莎·努斯鲍姆:"模仿专家",《新共和》第22卷,1999年第2期,第38页。

7. 努斯鲍姆:"模仿专家",第40页。

8. 努斯鲍姆:"模仿专家",第38页。

9. 参见艾琳·黛尔蒙德和李·昆比编:《女权主义与福柯:关于抵制的种种看法》,波士顿:东北大学出版社,1988年,第7页。

12 未来展望

要点 ⚷

- 福柯的《性史（第一卷）》仍然影响着当代学术界，尤其是最近有关治理术和全球化（跨越大陆边界的经济、文化和政府联系的紧密化）的学术讨论。

- 福柯的观点很可能会被长期用于讨论同性恋婚姻和同性恋权利，以及各个时代的社会权力结构的学术研究中。

- 《性史（第一卷）》标志着人文社科历史上的一个重要突破，彰显了知识本身被生产的本质，以及学术分析是由其所在文化和历史背景所塑造。

潜力

米歇尔·福柯的《性史（第一卷）：求知意志》对于新的社会、历史条件以及其他连福柯都未曾预料到的问题都有着重要的现实意义。例如，社会理论家安东尼奥·内格里和迈克尔·哈特*的《帝国》（2000）一书，采用福柯的生命政治*概念和生命权力概念来追溯从传统的王权统治和民族国家向由跨国公司和跨国政府组织（如联合国*）构成的世界秩序的转变。[1]

在《性史（第一卷）》中，福柯认为，他所称的"生命政治"权力旨在规范社会生活，而围绕性存在使用的语言则是其中最重要的一种体现方式。内格里和哈特修改了福柯的观点，他们认为性存在并不是今天规范社会生活的重要主题；相反，生命政治控制与全球化的经济进程有关。这种对福柯论点的改变部分反映了这样一个现实，即西方的性少数群体受到的待遇与 20 世纪 70 年代中期《性史（第一卷）》出版时相比有所改善。但或许更重要的是，这种改变体现了福柯思想具有丰富性和灵活性，至今仍可以被用来考察他在世时才初露苗头的论题（比如全球化）。

> "当我读到'知识就是权力'或'权力就是知识'的文章时——我知道人们认为这些话是我说的——我不禁开怀大笑，因为研究这两者的关系正是我的研究关键所在。如果这两者是相同的，我就不必研究它们，也能免于很多辛苦。事实是，我提出这两者关系作为研究主题的本身，就证明了我并没有将它们视为相同的概念。"
>
> —— 米歇尔·福柯，引自热拉尔·罗莱：《结构主义和后结构主义：米歇尔·福柯访谈》

未来方向

福柯的作品仍然是学术界和公众对性别、性存在、女权主义和同性恋运动等主题进行探讨所采用的重要参考。特别是在酷儿理论和性别与性存在研究等领域，他的作品具有很高的知名度和认可度，可一直作为大学课程和新的出版物的参考。正如文化理论家塔姆辛·斯帕戈在《福柯和酷儿理论》（1999）一书中所指出的那样，福柯本人和他关于性的作品"为许多男同性恋、女同性恋和知识分子树立了有力典范"。[2] 因此，我们可以得到这样的结论：作为有关讨论性取向和性别认同定义和分类（并质疑这些分类是否有必要）的关键文本，《性史（第一卷）》将持续发挥其价值。

例如，过去十年来美国同性恋婚姻合法化的讨论中常常使用福柯的观点佐证，恰好说明目前和未来关于男同性恋、女同性恋和跨性别者＊（那些认为出生时的性别不符合自己心理性别的人）权利的讨论上，福柯的观点将一直拥有现实意义。在《福柯—马克思主义冲突：同性恋婚姻中的剥削与权力》（2006）一书中，评论家尼克·斯通指出，福柯"会更加关注当前关于同性婚姻争辩的普遍性而不是同性婚姻问题本身，因为这场辩论的本质就是对他关于压抑和性的理论的部分证实。"[3] 他认为《性史（第一卷）》提供了一种关于同性恋婚姻如何演变的思考方法，包括支持者和反对者如何构建他们的论点，以及该问题在公共辩论中的重要性，并指出"在两次涉外战争和严重的经济困境中，同性恋问题仍然引起全国的关注，这一点佐证了福柯的论点：西方社会难以避免对自身性存在话题的讨论。"[4]

福柯的生命政治概念也在继续被学界使用。其中最值得注意的是意大利哲学家乔治·阿甘本＊的"神圣之人系列书籍"，第一册写于 20 世纪 90 年代中期。到目前为止，他已经完成了该系列七本书的创作，包括《神圣之人》（1995）、《例外状况》（2003）以及最近的《最高贫困：修道院规则和生命形式》（2013）。此系列的最后一本是一部关于 4 世纪的书面规则如何产生以及如何发展成为法律的谱系研究，完全基于福柯的论述精神。正如福柯对同性婚姻观点的讨论一样，阿甘本的论述展示了如何采用福柯的思想讨论新的问题。

小结

《性史（第一卷）》是人文社科领域的重要作品。福柯推翻了人们长期以来持有的"18、19 世纪社会普遍性压抑"的观点。但他也表示，这种观点仅仅是主流观念的变异，比如自 18 世纪以来，精神病学和生物学等学科不断推动，一直在鼓励人们对性作出语言表述。也就是说，他揭示了起初研究并规范性行为的机制后来也同样创造了围绕性解放展开的讨论。

福柯的作品为许多研究领域奠定了基础，包括性别和性存在研究、酷儿理论和治理研究。人们应该特别关注目前在政治、教育、性存在和社会运动的各类讨论中福柯作品所占据的中心地位。他的作品涵盖并影响多个学科，从文学、哲学到社会学、人类学。

然而，正如标题提醒我们的，《性史（第一卷）》须从历史角度来考量。虽然历史学教授艾伦·梅吉尔认为，"他与历史（学科）之间差别甚远，"[5] 但福柯的作品引起了历史学家们的激烈争鸣。[6] 他提出历史无法得到整体解读，更别说以统一的方式叙述了。相反，他展示了我们根深蒂固的信念如何影响我们对过去的理解，使我们只能以一种方式去解读。通过揭示西方科学家如何研究性存在，并在这些研究的基础上建立分类、规范和规则，福柯还论述了知识在多大程度上影响文化、塑造身份认同并维护权力结构。这些思想对于他所处的时代来说十分新颖，将继续影响学者们关于权力、治理和知识的辩论。

---

1. 迈克尔·哈特和安东尼奥·内格里：《帝国》，坎布里奇：哈佛大学出版社，2000 年。

2. 塔姆辛·斯帕戈：《福柯与酷儿理论》，剑桥：图标出版社，1999 年，第 8 页。

3. 尼克·斯通："福柯—马克思主义的冲突：同性婚姻中的剥削与权力"，《发现》

第 7 卷，2006 年，第 66 页，登录日期 2015 年 11 月 15 日，http://www.arts.cornell.edu/knight_institute/publicationsprizes/discoveries/discoveriesspring2006/06stone.pdf。

4. 斯通："福柯—马克思主义的冲突"，第 70 页。

5. 艾伦·梅吉尔："历史学家对福柯的反响"，《观念史杂志》第 48 卷，1987 年，第 117 页。

6. 马克·波斯特：《福柯、马克思主义与历史：生产方式与信息方式》，剑桥：政体出版社，1984 年。

术语表

1. **艾滋病（获得性免疫缺陷综合征）**：由艾滋病毒（人类免疫缺陷病毒）引起的疾病，最初于1959年在刚果发现，1981年在美国也发现病例。福柯死于艾滋病。他和他关于性存在的作品影响了20世纪80年代的社会活动家们，他们试图传播对这一疾病的认识并推翻"只有男同性恋者才有可能被感染"的错误观点。

2. **无政府主义政治理论**：政治理论的一个分支，通过非等级制度（有时也称为无国家社会）提倡自治。

3. **男性中心主义**：专注于男性的经验。

4. **年鉴派**：20世纪法国主要围绕着期刊《年鉴：经济、社会、文明》发展起来的一种撰写历史的方法和风格。该期刊使用社会科学的方法来关注社会而非外交或政治问题。

5. **人类学**：对人类、人类行为及其文化的研究。该领域受到了物理学、生物学、社会科学和人文学科的许多其他领域的影响。

6. **反本质主义**：拒绝承认人或事物中存在自然本质或既定身份的知识传统（例如，福柯主张性认同不是本能的，而是由社会建构的）。

7. **《知识考古学》（1969）**：米歇尔·福柯的一部著作。考古学分析文物和遗迹，以了解过去的人类活动和他们生活的社会。福柯在书中使用了这个词，并在他学术生涯的前半部分以此指代他的历史研究方法：通过剖析过去的话语和体系存留下的痕迹，可以让我们理解我们之所以成为今天的我们的过程。

8. **色情作品（快乐艺术）**：一个拉丁术语，福柯用来指将性作为一种艺术形式的观点，区别于将性作为知识对象的西方科学分析方法，比如性学。

9. **生物人类学**：人类学的一个分支，研究与进化历史和生物学相关的人类进化和生态学，并假设人类行为部分植根于某些先天的、遗传的特征。这些观点与福柯的理论不一致，后者假设所有人类行为是社会建构的。

10. **生物学**：研究生命体的自然科学，包括生物体的功能、结构、生长、进化、分类和分布。

11. **生命政治**：福柯创造的术语，用来描述那些旨在规范和控制大众的生活的政治战略。他认为生命政治是现代社会典型的治理类型。

12. **生命权力**：福柯在《性史》中创造的一个术语，用来描述"为了征服身体和控制国民而导致众多不同技术的激增"。该术语描述了国家如何通过规范健康、性存在、遗传等来控制国民。

13. **《临床医学的诞生》**（1963）：福柯的早期著作之一。该书通过临床医学的创建来剖析现代医学的历史，以便考察病理（疾病）如何分类以及文化和习俗如何影响我们对健康的理解。与福柯的所有作品一样，该书关注知识和真理如何被构建。

14. **资产阶级**：古典马克思主义理论中用来指资本主义经济中拥有生产资料的人——土地所有者、工厂所有者和其他雇主。这些拥有生产资料的人又对下层阶级的工人（无产阶级）行使权力。资产阶级一般被认为滥用权力，剥削无产阶级（劳动人民）。

15. **资本主义**：一种经济体系，其中生产资料、贸易和工业是私人拥有的，所有的商业行为均出于私人利益。

16. **殖民主义**：指一个国家对另一个国家的统治，涉及统治者（殖民国家）和被统治者（殖民地）之间不平等的权力关系，以及利用殖民地资源来加强殖民者本国经济的剥削式做法。

17. **文化研究**：20世纪60年代在英国发展起来的学术流派，并随后在国际上广为传播。文化研究提出了对社会关系的人类学解读，将文化视为一种生活经验形式。

18. **人口统计学**：通常使用统计数据来研究特定人类社区的生活条件的学科，社区的范畴可以是城市、国家、邻里以及监狱或大学等特定机构。

19. 《规训与惩罚》(1975)：福柯的著作，探讨现代西方刑罚制度的沿革。

20. **认识论**：用于指知识研究、获取知识的方法和知识的基础。

21. **本质主义**：认为所有实体——包括动物、人类、人群、物体、观念——都具有对其身份和功能所必需的某些品质。福柯的著作是反本质主义的，因为它们质疑是否真的存在"人性"，是否所有人都拥有特定的人类本质。

22. **欧洲中心主义**：一种思想倾向，认为欧洲文化比其他文化更优越或更重要。在学术研究中，欧洲中心主义的文章仅从欧洲的角度来看世界，不承认或考虑其他文化的角度。

23. **女权主义**：一系列意识形态和运动，意在让妇女获得平等的社会、政治、文化和经济权利，包括家庭、工作场所、教育和政府中的权利平等。

24. **女权主义、酷儿、男同性恋和女同性恋研究**：这些领域都探讨了社会和社会规范塑造性别、性和性取向的方式。

25. **弗洛伊德—马克思主义**：将马克思主义对资本主义的批判与弗洛伊德精神分析相结合的理论方法。最著名的弗洛伊德—马克思主义思想家包括赫伯特·马尔库塞和威廉·赖希。

26. **性别认同**：一个人对其性别的个体体验，即是男性还是女性，属于男性还是女性的类别。一个人可能对性别认同有一个模糊的概念，或者不确定其性别认同。

27. **性别研究**：研究性别是如何被社会所构建的。性别指代表"男性"或"女性"等身份的属性总和。

28. **谱系**：福柯使用德国哲学家尼采的"谱系"概念来描述他的历史研究方法。谱系剖析社会环境中的概念和实践，而不寻找它们的起源或内在真理。相反，它考察这些实践的相互关联性、相互依赖性，即某种实践会影响和塑造其他实践的结果。

29. **治理术**：旨在塑造公民行为而不是公开压制公民行为的治理实践。

福柯创造了这个术语，以帮助我们理解权力如何在现代社会中发挥作用。

30. **治理学研究**：应用福柯的治理术概念来理解治理在现代自由社会中的运作方式，包括医疗保健、移民和庇护问题，以及如何遏制犯罪。

31. **大拒绝**：赫伯特·马尔库塞的一个关键概念，指的是反对和抗议不必要的镇压，以及争取最终自由形式的斗争。这种最终自由形式指的是"没有焦虑地生活"。

32. **雌雄同体**：用于指在同一个人的身体中男性和女性器官同时存在或以两者组合的形式存在。

33. **异性恋常规性／异性恋**：认为所有人都可以被划分到明确的性别分类（男人和女人），这些性别分类具有与生俱来的相应角色，而且认为异性恋是唯一正常或自然的性取向。

34. **异性恋**：受到异性的性和／或爱情吸引。

35. **艾滋病病毒（HIV）**：人类免疫缺陷病毒，导致艾滋病的病毒性病原体。

36. **《性史（第二卷）》**（1984）：福柯关于性存在的研究著作的第二卷，研究了古希腊的性存在，特别关注愉悦的概念，以及愉悦的社会角色和对它的规范。

37. **《性史（第三卷）》**（1984）：福柯关于性存在的研究著作的第三卷，也是最后一卷。该书研究了古罗马的性存在，特别关注自我保健的概念。

38. **同性恋**：受到同性的性和／或爱情的吸引。

39. **人文学科**：用于定义与人类文化研究相关的学科的广义术语，包括历史、文学和文学批评、人类学、经典研究、地理、语言、法律、音乐、戏剧、舞蹈、哲学、宗教和视觉文化（电影、绘画、雕塑、游戏）。

40. **歇斯底里**：19世纪用来描述心理压力的身体表现的术语，最常见

于女性。福柯考察了该术语的起源及其在控制女性性欲等方面的作用。

41. **父亲法则**：法国精神分析学家和哲学家雅克·拉康创造的术语，用来描述禁止乱伦的法则，该法则将儿童引入规范社会纽带的规则体系和禁令体系。

42. **左派**：用于指持有左翼政治观点的个人或群体，也可指左翼政治观点。左翼观点倾向于倡导变革和改革，以促进平等。

43. **自由女权主义**：女权主义的个人主义分支，相信女性可以通过个人行为和选择获得平等。

44. **自由主义**：这个术语在经济学、社会和国际关系等领域具有不同内涵。在社会意义上，"自由主义"指的是倡导公民自由和个人权利，以及旨在改善民主和个人自由的政治改革；从经济学意义上讲，它指的是资本主义的市场自由原则。

45. **语言学家**：语言学的研究者（研究语言的性质、功能和结构）。

46. **《疯癫与文明》**（1964）：米歇尔·福柯的早期著作，研究现代精神失常概念的起源，并将其与启蒙运动后科学思想的发展联系起来。福柯的终极目标是展示我们对心理疾病理解的社会文化根源。

47. **马克思主义**：围绕着 19 世纪哲学家和经济学家卡尔·马克思的著作建立起来的思想和政治运动。

48. **五月风暴**：1968 年 5 月，法国发生大规模的内乱，包括抗议、罢工、占领学校和工厂以及骚乱，这一运动是由马克思主义思想中关于谋求更公正社会的号召所引发的。

49. **医学凝视**：福柯用来指代医生在治疗患者时所采用的去人性化的临床方法，包括将身体和心理视为独立的部分来治疗。

50. **中世纪**：用于指罗马帝国沦陷（大约在公元 500 年）和文艺复兴时期（14 世纪）之间的欧洲历史时期。

51. **现代性**：知识分子对 17 世纪后期发生的社会文化变革的回应，这

些社会文化变革包括工业化、城市的发展、民族国家的崛起和政治民主。这一概念常与基于科学、理性和自由主义的新理念取代传统价值观和信念的过程密不可分。

52. **新自由主义**：一种政治经济学理论和实践，推崇创业自由、私有化和放松市场管制，同时减少对社会福利的关注。

53. **神经学**：对大脑和神经系统的研究。

54. 《**论道德的谱系：一个论战**》（1887）：弗里德里希·尼采的一部著作，其中描述了道德概念的起源。福柯的大部分作品都是基于或阐释尼采文本中提出的思想。

55. 《**词与物：人文科学考古学**》（1966）：米歇尔·福柯的一部著作，试图借用考古学的语言来挖掘人类科学（特别是社会学和心理学）的起源。与福柯的其他著作一样，该书首先关注知识的构建方式和我们对真理的假设；然而，该书采用的结构主义方法与后期作品的方法不同。

56. **正统马克思主义**：指对马克思（著作）的狭义阐释，主要与经济学在社会关系中的突出作用有关。

57. **病理**：用来描述任何心理或身体失调或不适的广义术语。病理行为是指反映潜在精神障碍的行为。福柯的许多著作都关注病理的定义以及这些定义所揭示的周遭文化。

58. **父权制**：由男性统治的社会组织（政府、家庭和其他社区），其中血统划入父系，儿童被赋予父亲的姓氏。

59. **教育学**：教学实践和教育所依据的理论或原则。

60. **现象学**：18世纪发展起来的哲学分支，研究经验结构和我们对周围世界感知的意识结构，以及感知在我们的认知方式中所扮演的角色。

61. **多态的**：呈现或具有纷杂多变的形式、特征或风格，或以纷杂多变的形式、特征或风格出现的东西。福柯声称权力是"多态的"，因为它呈现出不同的形式。

62. **实证主义**：一种哲学学派，认为观察到的东西可以成为人类认知的合理来源。通过强调经验（基于实验或观察的经验）以及持有特定"真理"的经验，实证主义学者通常不考虑主体是如何通过文化、意识形态和语言来得到调节和定义的。

63. **后殖民研究**：一门学科，研究殖民地在政治"独立"之前或之后，殖民主义和帝国主义对前殖民地的文化和人口有何影响。它受到一系列学科和思想流派的影响，特别是后结构主义、批判理论、马克思主义理论和人类学。

64. **后马克思主义**：一种以马克思主义为基础的社会理论和哲学，它延伸、逆转或修改马克思主义思想。经常使用福柯论点的当代后马克思主义者包括埃内斯托·拉克劳、尚泰尔·慕菲和安东尼奥·内格里。

65. **后结构主义**：主要指的是20世纪60年代和70年代的法国理论家和哲学家的作品，他们认为社会结构和各种分类基本上是不稳定的。尽管福柯经常被认为是后结构主义者，但他拒绝这样的标签。

66. **监狱情报小组**：1971年在法国成立的团体，试图将监狱的情况在收音机和报纸上报道，以揭露监狱里的环境条件。该团体出版了四本期刊，试图"将监狱内的情况彻底曝光"，通过信息发布，试图让监狱官员而不是囚犯成为受关注的目标。

67. **精神病学**：从事精神障碍的研究、治疗和预防的医学分支。

68. **精神分析**：西格蒙德·弗洛伊德在19世纪晚期构想的理论和方法，旨在理解人类的心理和治疗精神障碍。

69. **心理学**：一门学术和应用学科，研究和治疗心理行为和心理功能。

70. **酷儿理论**：20世纪90年代在北美人文学科中出现的学术领域，之后主要在英语学术界传播。酷儿理论旨在挑战传统的性向分类和其他方面的分类。

71. **压抑假设**：米歇尔·福柯的《性史（第一卷）》其中一章的标题。他在整本书中使用了这个术语来描述在历史上一整套关于性存在的角色的特定信念，这个假说由弗洛伊德—马克思主义学者在20

世纪 60 年代和 70 年代进一步发展，五月风暴之后，性解放倡导者
也推动了它的发展。

72. **罗马天主教忏悔圣事**：一种宗教仪式，个人告诉牧师他或她的罪
（违背基督教教义的事），并请求上帝的宽恕。

73. **罗马天主教**：一个广义术语，指的是罗马天主教会的特有传统，包
括（但不限于）他们的教义、伦理和神学。

74. **性存在研究**：探讨整个社会在电影、艺术、流行文化、文学和政治
等领域如何构建性身份的学术领域。

75. **性取向**：用于指一个人的性别认同的术语，可通过个人被何种性别
所吸引来判断其性取向。异性恋、同性恋和双性恋都是性取向。

76. 社会科学：一个广泛的术语，指考察社会和人类关系的学科群，包
括经济学、历史、法律、心理学、社会学、政治学、教育学、地
理学和人类学。

77. 社会学：社会行为的学术研究。该学科考察了社会关系的起源和发
展以及多种多样的组织模式和社会制度。

78. 结构主义：一种理论方法，认为必须将文化元素放在与它们所属
的较大结构和系统的关系之中，才能理解这些文化元素。该理论
起源于语言学家费尔迪南·索绪尔，后来由人类学家克劳德·列
维—斯特劳斯等学者进一步发展。

79. 主体性：用于解释个体之间差异（包括品味、观点、价值观和信
仰）的概念，并说明一个人的观点与周围群体的观点之间的差距。
在哲学中，这个概念对于讨论"为什么人们解释、看待周围世界
的方式会如此不同"至关重要。

80. **神学**：对宗教观念的系统研究，通常通过阅读经文来进行分析。

81. **跨性别者**：跨性别者认为自己在出生时所获得的性别（基于他们的
生殖器）是不正确的。跨性别者可以选择进行变性手术和激素治
疗，以成为他们认为自己应该具有的性别。

82. **联合国**：第二次世界大战后设立的国际机构，旨在促进国家间的交流、合作和安全，其总部设在纽约。

83. **维多利亚时代的道德观**：1837 年至 1901 年维多利亚女王统治时期的道德价值观。这些道德价值观涉及严格的社会行为规则，如性约束和禁止低俗语言等。

84. **越南战争**（1955—1975）：北越和南越之间发生的武装冲突，老挝和柬埔寨也卷入其中。法国对越南战争的介入遭到国内反对，这是引发法国五月风暴的因素之一。

85. **权力意志**：弗里德里希·尼采发展的一个重要概念，他认为人类的动力是权力意志：获得最高地位的野心和渴望。

86. **第一次世界大战**（1914—1918）：同盟国（德国和奥匈帝国）和协约国（俄罗斯帝国、大英帝国和法国）之间的世界级战争。

人名表

1. 乔治·阿甘本（1942年生），当代重要的意大利哲学家和政治理论家，从事语言学、法律和政治领域的工作。他最著名的作品包括《神圣之人》（1998）和《例外状况》（2005）。

2. 路易斯·阿尔都塞（1918—1990），法国马克思主义哲学家。虽然今天人们通常将他与结构主义学派联系在一起，但他对结构主义思想的某些方面持批评态度，而且一生都在支持马克思主义的核心原则。福柯深受阿尔都塞作品的影响。

3. 朱迪斯·巴特勒（1956年生），非常有影响力的美国理论家和学者。她的作品极大地影响了女权主义和酷儿理论等研究领域。她最著名的作品包括《性别麻烦》（1990）和《身体之重》（1993）。

4. 詹姆斯·克利福德（1945年生），美国人类学家。

5. 雅克·德里达（1930—2004），法国哲学家，因"解构"方面的著作以及积极参与结构主义和后结构主义学派而闻名。"解构"是一种符号学分析方法。德里达和福柯在批评方法上极不相同，据说福柯的一些著作是针对德里达批评的直接回应。

6. 爱比克泰德（55—135），讲希腊语的哲学家，生活在罗马。他将哲学作为一种生活方式，而不仅仅是一种理论学科。福柯在《性史（第三卷）》中经常提到爱比克泰德关于道德、死亡、独立和自我的观点。

7. 西格蒙德·弗洛伊德（1856—1939），奥地利神经学家。他开创了一种观点，认为人类的行为在很大程度上是由无意识的欲望和原始的冲动所驱使的。他是精神分析的创始人。

8. 大卫·M.哈尔珀林（1952年生），美国学者，专业方向为酷儿理论、酷儿研究、批判理论、视觉文化和物质文化等。他最出名的著作是《同性恋一百年》（1990），书中他论述了理查德·冯·克拉夫特—埃宾在性病理学研究著作《性心理疾病》中使用"同性恋"

这一术语的历史意义。《性心理疾病》的英译本于 1892 年出版。哈尔珀林撰写了大量关于福柯及其对酷儿研究影响的文章。

9. **迈克尔·哈特**（1960 年生），美国马克思主义 / 后马克思主义文学理论家和政治哲学家。他最著名的作品是与安东尼·内格里共同撰写的《帝国》（2000）。这本书运用福柯的生命权力和生命政治概念来研究权力如何在冷战后的全球化经济中运作。

10. **托马斯·赫希霍恩**（1957 年生），瑞士艺术家，以其政治性的艺术装置作品而闻名。他的很多装置作品向开创性的左翼思想家致敬。迄今为止，安东尼奥·葛兰西、吉尔·德勒兹和米歇尔·福柯都给他的作品提供过灵感。他的"福柯 24 小时"是一个艺术装置作品，其中包括图书馆、商店、酒吧和礼堂等，旨在为观众创造一个类似于福柯大脑内部的空间。

11. **让·伊波利特**（1907—1968），法国哲学家，黑格尔和德国哲学运动的追随者，20 世纪中期法国思想的杰出人物。福柯在他的指导下学习，并深受他对历史与哲学之间关系的看法的影响。

12. **雅克·拉康**（1901—1981），法国精神分析学家和精神病学家，他以提倡"回归弗洛伊德"而著名。他通过仔细阅读弗洛伊德的文本，纠正了其追随者对其理论的误解和歪曲（尤其是在美国）。拉康精神分析对法国哲学和女权主义理论产生了深远的影响。

13. **埃内斯托·拉克劳**（1935—2014），阿根廷后马克思主义政治理论家。他最出名的著作是与尚泰尔·慕非合著的《文化霸权和社会主义战略》（1985）以及他的第一本书《马克思主义理论中的政治与意识形态》（1977）。拉克劳受到了福柯有关权力的著作的极大影响。

14. **克劳德·列维-斯特劳斯**（1908—2009），法国人种学家和人类学家，常被称为"现代人类学之父"。他的作品将费尔迪南·德·索绪尔的结构语言学理论应用在人类学中。

15. **赫伯特·马尔库塞**（1898—1979），颇有影响力的德国哲学家，生活在美国，也是法兰克福学派的杰出成员，致力于研究马克思主义和精神分析的交集。他最著名的作品包括《爱欲与文明》（1955）

和《单向度的人》（1964）。

16. 毕蒂·马丁（1951年生），美国作家和知识分子，因其关于女权主义和酷儿理论的著作而闻名。最值得一提的作品是《女权主义者直言：女同性恋的重要意义》（1996）。马丁一直批评福柯的作品，认为他对性存在的观点以男性为中心，并不适合女权主义的应用。

17. 卡尔·马克思（1818—1883），德国政治哲学家和经济学家，他对资本主义制度内阶级关系的分析和对平等主义制度的阐述为共产主义提供了基础。马克思与弗里德里希·恩格斯（1820—1895）一起撰写了《共产党宣言》（1848）。他在《资本论》（1867）中阐述了他关于生产和阶级关系的完整理论。

18. 莫里斯·梅洛-庞蒂（1908—1961），法国现象学哲学家和作家，也是他那个时代唯一一位将描述心理学纳入其作品讨论的主要哲学家。这影响了后来的现象学家，他们在研究中使用了认知科学和心理学。

19. 尚泰尔·慕非（1943年生），比利时政治理论家，最著名的成就是与埃内斯托·拉克劳一起发展了话语分析。这是一种后马克思主义政治探究的方法，它借鉴了后结构主义思想，包括福柯的观念。她和拉克劳共同撰写了《文化霸权和社会主义战略》（1985），这本书被认为是奠定了话语分析的基础。

20. 安东尼奥·内格里（1933年生），意大利马克思主义/后马克思主义哲学家，因他与迈克尔·哈特合著的《帝国》（2000）而闻名。内格里在他的大部分作品中都应用了福柯的生命权力和生命政治概念。

21. 弗里德里希·尼采（1844—1900），杰出的德国哲学家，他从根本上质疑宗教、道德和真理等概念。

22. 玛莎·努斯鲍姆（1947年生），美国哲学家，她是芝加哥大学讲授法律和道德的教授。

23. 莫妮克·普拉扎，法国女权主义作家和思想家，颇具影响力的法国期刊《女性主义问题》的联合创始人，该期刊于1980年首次出版。

普拉扎对福柯思想提出了直言不讳的批评。

24. **普罗塔克**（约46—约120），希腊散文家、历史学家和传记作家。福柯在《性史（第三卷）》一书中提到了普罗塔克关于爱与性的著作。

25. **威廉·赖希**（1897—1957），激进的奥地利精神分析家，他围绕性压抑造成的影响撰写了大量作品。他最著名的作品包括《法西斯主义的大众心理学》（1933）和《性革命》（1936）。

26. **尼古拉斯·罗斯**（1947年生），颇具影响力的英国社会理论家和社会学家。他的作品关注心理健康政策和风险、精神病学的社会学和历史以及心理健康领域精神药理学发展的社会影响。他最出名的就是他有关福柯的著作，以及在英语国家中掀起对福柯有关治理概念的兴趣。

27. **费尔迪南·德·索绪尔**（1857—1913），瑞士语言学家，他对语言结构的看法为20世纪的语言科学奠定了基础。

28. **艾伦·D.斯克里夫特**，美国爱荷华州格林内尔学院教授，讲授19世纪和20世纪法国和德国哲学。他撰写了大量关于福柯的著作。

29. **伊芙·塞奇威克**（1950—2009），颇具影响力的美国理论家，酷儿理论和性别研究领域的大学教授。她最著名的作品是《暗柜认识论》（1990）。

30. **塞内卡**（公元前4年—公元65年），罗马哲学家，尼禄皇帝的导师，斯多葛主义哲学学派的支持者。福柯在《性史（第三卷）》中讨论过他。福柯关于塞内卡"关心自我"的观点的讨论使学者们重新思考对他作品的评价。

31. **塔姆辛·斯帕戈**，文化历史学家，专门研究酷儿理论、酷儿文化、性别和反文化文学。

32. **佳亚特里·斯皮瓦克**（1942年生），印度理论家和哲学家，她的作品在后殖民研究领域具有极大的影响力。她最被广泛阅读的作品之一是《底层人能说话吗？》（1988）。

33. **安·斯托勒**（1949 年生），美国人类学家，以其关于帝国性政治的著作（殖民统治下如何对待性存在和性别）以及关于殖民统治问题的作品而闻名。她是第一批指出福柯在关于现代西方文化中性存在的论述中未能提到一个关键因素——殖民主义——的学者之一。

34. **法蒂·特里基**（1947 年生），法国哲学家，突尼斯大学的荣誉教授。他在福柯的指导下学习，并受到福柯思想的极大影响。

35. **卡尔·韦斯特法尔**（1833—1890），德国精神病学家，最著名的贡献是创造了术语"恐旷症"（又译"广场恐惧症"）。"恐旷症"指对大型开放空间的恐惧。福柯还将"同性恋"一词的创造归功于韦斯特法尔。这个词影响了现代同性恋的定义，即与某人身份相关的东西。韦斯特法尔认为同性恋是一种精神疾病。

36. **大卫·沃纳洛维奇**（1954—1992），同性恋艺术家、作家、电影制作人、摄影师和艾滋病活动家，活跃于 20 世纪 70 年代和 80 年代的纽约艺术圈。他的艺术装置作品经常会引起争议，这些作品试图挑战大众对同性恋和艾滋病的污名化。酷儿理论家常将他放在福柯著作的背景中进行讨论。

WAYS IN TO THE TEXT

- Michel Foucault is among the twentieth century's most influential social scientists; he wrote widely on the relationship between knowledge and power.

- Foucault's *The History of Sexuality Vol. 1* (1976) challenged then-widespread views about sexuality and sexual repression, and offered a new approach to understanding the relationship between sexuality, knowledge, and power.

- *The History of Sexuality* changed the way scholars talked about sex and sexuality, and paved the way for a host of new academic disciplines, including gender studies* (inquiry into the ways that gender—the sum of attributes considered to represent identities such as "male" or "female"—are constituted by society) and queer theory* (an approach to cultural analysis that begins by acknowledging the instability and uncertainty of sexual identity and knowledge itself).

Who Was Michel Foucault?

Michel Foucault (1926–84), the author of *The History of Sexuality Vol. 1: The Will to Knowledge*, was a French philosopher, historian, and writer. He is best known as the author of *The Birth of the Clinic* (1963) (a study of the history of medicine), of *Madness and Civilization* (1964), and of a study of the modern prison, *Discipline and Punish* (1975). His *History of Sexuality* was originally intended as the first of a six-volume examination of how sex has been understood throughout history.

Foucault was interested in how different systems of knowledge originate, and how knowledge is used to control, regulate, and even shape people's identities. His work explores the nature of the power associated with knowledge, and how knowledge systems evolve over time.

In 1976, when he published *Sexuality Vol. 1*, Foucault was already a respected intellectual with a global reputation. In 1969 he was appointed professor at the *Collège de France*, a prestigious higher education institution in Paris (professorships there are reserved for highly established academics). He chose for himself the title Historian of Systems of Thought. As a professor, Foucault was responsible for giving an annual series of lectures on the theme of his choice. One of them was the subject that became the first volume of his *History of Sexuality*. Foucault died of an AIDS*-related illness in 1984, shortly after the publication of *Vol. 2** and *Vol. 3.**

What Does *The History of Sexuality Vol. 1* Say?

Foucault looks at the ways in which sex has been talked about in the modern Western world. Since the Middle Ages* (approximately the sixth to the fourteenth centuries), he claims that Western societies have increasingly turned to the practice of Roman Catholic* confession* as a means of putting sexual practices and desires into words (in confession, Roman Catholic Christians confess their sins to a priest in exchange for forgiveness). This argument went against a commonly held view among scholars of his time that sex—particularly in the nineteenth century—was not talked about, and that the Church and the state tried to prevent all mention of it.

Foucault also believes that calls for sexual liberation are

related to the fact that sex has been talked about a great deal in modern times. He makes his argument in contrast to what he calls the "repressive hypothesis."* According to this theory, which was often behind the loud calls for sexual liberation in the 1960s and 1970s, natural expressions of sexuality have been repressed and silenced by the bourgeoisie* (the rich and powerful class of business owners). Foucault says this idea developed from Victorian attitudes to sex (the straightlaced approach that characterized the reign of Britain's Queen Victoria from 1837 to 1901), which were commonly seen as having been restricted and repressed.

Foucault contrasts the open attitudes toward sex of the seventeenth century with those of the Victorian period, but he maintains that, contrary to what people believed, the Victorians did not hide sex behind closed doors. Although they did try to stop talking about sex, in practice they were not very successful. This is a valuable part of Foucault's analysis. He maintains that during the eighteenth and nineteenth centuries sex was talked about a lot, and was even turned into an object of scientific study. A complex scientific conversation arose around sexuality that led to the identification of certain pathologies* (or types of disorders), such as the homosexual,* the hysterical* woman, or the masturbating child. This information was then used to establish definitions and theories about normal and abnormal behavior and, in turn, to create laws to regulate sexuality.

However, according to Foucault, this discourse (that is, discussion) around sex accepted various sexualities and treated them as legitimate. Moreover, this attitude was not directly imposed on the lower classes (the wage earners and small farmers) by the dominant class (the bourgeoisie or business owners). Instead, it was first developed to reassure the dominant class of its superiority before spreading to the lower classes.

By investigating sexual history and theory, Foucault concludes that power in modern societies is not enforced so much by suppression or direct domination (the use of force and violence). Instead, power over the population is exercised through complex and scattered techniques and mechanisms, mainly involving the production of knowledge, scientific or otherwise.

Why Does *The History of Sexuality Vol. 1* Matter?

Sexuality Vol. 1 changed the way scholars thought about sex and sexuality, power, and knowledge. It suggested a whole new approach to the study of sexuality that favored historical analysis rather than psychoanalysis,* (a therapeutic and theoretical approach to the unconscious mind developed by the Austrian thinker Sigmund Freud* in the late nineteenth century). It also introduced a new way of thinking about sex and power that complicated the simplistic explanations that were popular at the time.

The 1960s saw a profound change in attitudes toward sex. Those who supported sexual liberation, along with social science* and humanities* scholars, tended to see a conflict between an individual's instinctive desires and the various authorities that tried to limit it ("humanities" here refers to academic disciplines relating to the study of human culture, such as history and literature). Such authorities could be the government, the Church, or even a repressive parent or spouse. Those who shared this view thought that sexual liberation would only come about by allowing people to follow their sexual desires without being prevented by laws or social customs.

Foucault challenged this view, maintaining that both sexuality and power are far more complex than a strict division between instinct and authority would suggest. In making this claim, he opened up a new way of thinking about sex and sexuality, and paved the way for new disciplines such as gender and sexuality studies,* and new ideas such as queer theory, which helped broaden the debate around the social role of sex. The text continues to be an important work for anyone interested in gender and sexuality, and is significant for those seeking to understand Foucault's overall thinking.

SECTION 1
INFLUENCES

THE AUTHOR AND THE HISTORICAL CONTEXT

KEY POINTS

* *The History of Sexuality Vol. 1* was a groundbreaking work of philosophical and cultural criticism that changed the way scholars thought about sexuality and power.

* Foucault was shaped by his conservative upbringing and postwar France's repressive ideas about sexuality; in the 1960s and 1970s he was active in left-wing movements.

* While his own homosexuality* and liberal* views were at odds with the culture of his time, Foucault's ideas on sexuality were also at odds with those of the French left.

Why Read This Text?

Michel Foucault's *The History of Sexuality Vol. 1: The Will to Knowledge* is a study of the evolution of cultural ideas about sex. It examines how the idea of sexuality was used to regulate, control, and rule. Foucault argues that, since the end of the seventeenth century, the discussion of sex in Western culture grew across different branches of science, such as biology* (the study of living things), psychiatry* (the study and treatment of mental disorders), and pedagogy* (teaching). As an object of scientific knowledge, sexual preferences came to be seen as a problem of "truth" that could reveal something about a person's identity.

The core question Foucault sets out to answer is: "Why do we say, with so much passion and so much resentment against our most recent past, against our present, and against ourselves, that we are repressed?"[1] Throughout the book, and the following two volumes of the series, Foucault argues that a will to know and speak about sex affects the ways that our societies understand sexual desires and practices.

Sexuality Vol. 1 broke new ground. It changed the way scholars thought about sexuality and power. It also drew attention to the way that, over the centuries, rules about sex have been used to regulate citizens' behavior and uphold state power. Foucault came up with a new way of understanding the concept of power: it was, he said, "polymorphous"*—that is, something that takes many shapes, and invades all aspects of life, rather than something imposed by one ruler.

> "Since the end of the sixteenth century, the 'putting into discourse of sex,' far from undergoing a process of restriction, on the contrary has been subjected to a mechanism of increasing incitement … the will to knowledge has not come to a halt in the face of a taboo that must not be lifted, but has persisted in constituting—despite many mistakes, of course— a science of sexuality."
>
> —— Michel Foucault, *The History of Sexuality Vol. 1: The Will to Knowledge*

Author's Life

Michel Foucault was born in 1926 into an upper-middle class family in Poitiers, France. Resisting expectations to become a doctor like his father, he enrolled in the Lycée Henri-IV, a highly regarded secondary school in Paris, where he studied philosophy under the famous philosopher Jean Hyppolite.* 2 He then entered the *École Normale Supérieure d'Ulm* (ENS), the most prestigious French university for the humanities,* where he studied under the Marxist* philosopher Louis Althusser* (Marxism is a method of social and historical analysis founded on the thought of the nineteenth-century political philosopher Karl Marx).* He graduated with a degree in psychological sciences in 1948, and with a second degree in philosophy in 1951. While studying philosophy, he worked with the renowned phenomenologist* Maurice Merleau-Ponty.* (Phenomenology is the branch of philosophy that studies the structures that inform our experience and our consciousness of the world around us, and the role that perception plays in the way we relate to the world.)

Foucault openly stated that his books were not only influenced by the scholars he studied, but also by his personal experiences. Although his father came from a strict Roman Catholic* background (Roman Catholicism being the largest branch of the Christian faith), Foucault was not religious, and he was suspicious of beliefs that attempted to interpret the world in its entirety. This can, in part, explain his lasting concern with knowledge and power. Perhaps more importantly, as a gay man living in conservative postwar France, Foucault experienced firsthand an oppressive heteronormative* culture (a culture that accepts only heterosexuality* as the norm, and condemns homosexuality). Foucault attempted suicide in 1948 and was hospitalized in a psychiatric institution in Paris. His doctors diagnosed his later attempts to kill himself as reactions to the social stigma and shame attached to being openly gay.

At the time Foucault was writing *Sexuality Vol. 1*, he had already been appointed as a professor at the highly respected *Collège de France*, holding one of the highest academic positions in the country. The year following publication, he was invited to consult with the French government on changes to the laws dealing with rape.[3] Foucault was also politically active in left-wing movements throughout the 1970s. Most notably, he was a member of *Groupe d'Information sur les Prisons* (*Prison Information Group**), a group that fought for inmates' rights and distributed information about prisons. Foucault died in 1984 in Paris from an HIV*-related disease.

Author's Background

Foucault's concerns in *Sexuality Vol. 1,* as well as in his other works, were very much of their time. Although France in the 1970s was relatively stable, the previous decade had seen intense social upheaval. The country had endured several bitter conflicts, including opposition to its bloody but ultimately unsuccessful wars to keep its colonies (Vietnam won independence in 1954 but French activists laid the blame for the subsequent Vietnam War* on France's legacy in the area; Algeria won its independence in 1962), and what students saw as the elitism of the education system. There was also widespread anticapitalist* sentiment that gave rise to strikes and occupations across the land (capitalism is the social and economic system dominant in the West and increasingly throughout the world, in which trade and industry are conducted for private profit). This unrest climaxed with the events of May 1968,* during which students occupied the Sorbonne University, a prestigious and notably old seat of learning in Paris, to oppose the capitalist system and traditional values.

The students' occupation inspired the largest workers' strike the country had ever seen, during which the French economy effectively ground to a halt. Both the student occupation and the strike were finally put down with police force, and the events did little to change France's political structure. However, those two weeks of unrest came to be seen as a watershed moment. The women's rights movement in France began immediately after the events of 1968, and French feminism* and interest in sexuality as a concept grew over the course of the 1970s (feminism denotes the intellectual and political currents associated with the struggle for equality between the sexes).

This background provides important insight into the origins of Foucault's work. In particular, although Foucault participated in many of the leftist* movements of the 1960s, *Sexuality Vol. 1* does not endorse the views of the left concerning sex and sexuality. His objective in the book was in fact to challenge the arguments for sexual liberation common among leftist thinkers. The discussion of the period centered on the tension between people's instinctual sexual drives and the state powers or capitalist forces that sought to repress them. Foucault argued that this picture of oppressed and oppressors was overly simplistic, and he sought to complicate it.

1. Michel Foucault, *The History of Sexuality Vol. 1: The Will to Knowledge*, trans. Robert Hurley (London: Penguin Books, 1998), 8–9.

2. Daniel Defert, "Chronology," in *A Companion to Foucault*, eds. Christopher Falzon et al. (Chichester: Wiley & Sons, 2013), 11.

3. See Monique Plaza, "Our Costs and Their Benefits," in *Sex in Question: French Materialist Feminism*, eds. Diana Leonard and Lisa Adkins (London: Taylor & Francis, 1996), 184.

MODULE 2
ACADEMIC CONTEXT

KEY POINTS

- Foucault challenged the popular use of psychoanalytic* ideas to explain sexuality, rejecting the idea that people are born with their sexuality, and proposing that it is a result of social conditions.

- Foucault was associated with the structuralist* and poststructuralist* schools of thought, though he never accepted being part of either movement. (Structuralism and poststructuralism are approaches to the analysis of culture that differ on matters such as the extent to which we can be certain of objective knowledge.)

- Foucault was greatly influenced by the nineteenth-century German philosopher Friedrich Nietzsche.*

The Work in Its Context

After May 1968* Michel Foucault's *The History of Sexuality Vol. 1: The Will to Knowledge* entered into the debates taking place both in intellectual circles and in society in general (May 1968 was a time of radical social activism in Europe and the United States). In that era, the 1960s and 1970s, Western academic discussions of sex and sexuality were largely influenced by psychoanalytic thought.

Psychoanalysis began at the end of the nineteenth century. It was first developed by the Austrian neurologist* Sigmund Freud, who viewed a person's identity as formed by their unconscious desires and repressed childhood memories—memories people force themselves to forget since society considers them unacceptable (e.g., sexual love for a parent or the sight of one's own parents having sex). Freud argued that an individual's sexual identity was shaped by these experiences. In the 1960s and 1970s, social scientists, such as the German American philosopher Herbert Marcuse* and the Austrian psychoanalyst Wilhelm Reich,* introduced psychoanalytic concepts into their work. Foucault challenged their positions by offering a new way of thinking of sexuality, seeing it as an effect of social conditioning and not as something you are simply born with.

Foucault challenged psychoanalytic thought by claiming that a person's sexual orientation* or preference does not come so much from instinct and unconscious urges as from ideals learned in society. He writes that sexuality is organized around two ideas: "deviant" and "normal" sexual behaviors. For Foucault, this distinction helps separate sexual activities that a particular society considers acceptable (such as heterosexual,* reproductive sex within marriage) from those considered unacceptable (such as homosexual* activity and extramarital sex). Foucault argues that there is nothing natural or universal about these codes of behavior. Since society's view of what is deviant and what is considered normal changes over time, sexuality does as well. Put differently, sexuality is a product of changing sociohistorical circumstances and not unconscious drives, as claimed by psychoanalysis.

Moreover, Foucault argued that the psychoanalytic focus on talking about sexual repression was just another product of modern mechanisms of power. Psychoanalysis might claim that talking about sex openly could help unlock an individual's repressed experiences, but Foucault argued this view was itself a form of control, and not so different from the methods used by Victorian doctors to "cure" people of their sexual "perversions." The interest in talking about sex as a way to combat repression was common in France in the aftermath of May 1968. Foucault's resistance to such an approach was highly original.

> "What is peculiar to modern societies, in fact, is not that they consigned sex to a shadow existence, but that they dedicated themselves to speaking of it ad infinitum, while exploiting it as the secret."
>
> —— Michel Foucault, *The History of Sexuality Vol. 1: The Will to Knowledge*

Overview of the Field

As well as psychoanalysis, two other schools of thought—structuralism and poststructuralism—greatly influenced the course of twentieth-century thinking in the humanities* and social sciences,* and were also closely related to Foucault's work. In fact, his three-volume *History of Sexuality* (as well as his other writings) has been labeled structuralist and poststructuralist, even though Foucault himself resisted such labels.

Structuralism was developed after World War I* (1914–18) by scholars such as the Swiss linguist* Ferdinand de Saussure* and, later, the French anthropologist* Claude Lévi-Strauss* and the French philosopher Louis Althusser*—Foucault's teacher and a formative influence on his thinking. (Linguistics is the study of the nature and functioning of language, while anthropology is the study of human beings, especially our cultures, beliefs, and societies.) These thinkers believed that all culture is constructed—that is, the product of laws and unwritten rules that govern how people behave and what they believe. To understand any single element of culture, it was assumed, one must examine the institutions or whole social system of which it is a part.

Foucault's central point in *The History of Sexuality*—that sexuality is constructed by each society—can be understood as a structuralist approach. According to this view, all elements of culture exist—and are shaped by—their relation to larger ideas, institutions, and systems of their society.[1] In the same way, structuralism sees sexuality as something that is not the same for all societies, but rather depends on historical and cultural circumstances.

Poststructuralism was a movement that developed out of structuralism in the 1960s and 1970s, derived from the work of mostly French theorists and philosophers, such as Jacques Derrida.* These scholars regarded our understanding of social structures and categories as naturally unstable—that is, subject to change, and not very valid. They claimed that because all individuals are a product of their historical context, and are participants in their culture, no one could really examine *anything* "objectively," and without bias. Any scholar who examines a cultural artifact (anything made by people—and reflecting their culture) must, therefore, recognize that their own situation and background will to some extent influence their analysis. In this way, *The History of Sexuality* can also be read as a poststructuralist work in that its central aim is to disturb given categories and disprove stable definitions.[2]

While Foucault is often associated with poststructuralism, he was not a committed member of any particular school of thought. His historical approach and method is associated with the Annales School,* (an influential French school of historical inquiry that focused on social rather than diplomatic or political issues in studying history), but he never clearly stated that he was part of it.

Academic Influences

Foucault's work is highly indebted to the nineteenth-century German philosopher Friedrich Nietzsche. The approach that Foucault used in *Sexuality Vol. 1*, which he called "genealogical* critique," owes much to Nietzsche's *On the Genealogy of Morals** (1887).[3]

Genealogy, in philosophy, refers to the analysis of a historical period's different belief systems alongside each other, rather than individually. Rather than focusing on the origins of these systems, genealogy is interested in the conditions that allow them to exist (for example, the laws in place at the time). Foucault used this term to describe his own approach to historical analysis, which assumed all truths to be questionable and history itself to be a construct that can be endlessly revised as each generation offers a different viewpoint on the past that often contradicts the ideas of the generation before. *Sexuality Vol. 1*'s subtitle *The Will to Knowledge* refers to Nietzsche's "will to power,"* a term he used to describe what he believed was the motivating force in humans: ambition and the desire to achieve the highest possible position available to them. It also reflects Foucault's main aim: to analyze how the will to know and speak about sexuality forms itself and how it affects the ways our societies understand sexual practices.

Foucault admitted that Nietzsche was among his greatest influences, stating, "if I wanted to be pretentious, I would use 'the genealogy of morals' as the general title of what I am doing."[4] More generally, Foucault's interest in how scientists have examined sexuality as an object of knowledge reflects his lifelong aim to question modern structures and institutions.

---

1. Hubert L. Dreyfus and Paul Rabinow, eds., *Michel Foucault: Beyond Structuralism and Hermeneutics* (Chicago: University of Chicago Press, 1983); David H. J. Larmour et al., "Situating the *History of Sexuality,*" in *Rethinking Sexuality: Foucault and Classical Antiquity,* eds. David H. J. Larmour et al., (Princeton, New Jersey: Princeton University Press, 1998), 3–41.

2. See Nikki Sullivan, *A Critical Introduction to Queer Theory* (New York: NYU Press, 2003), 40.

3. See Friedrich Nietzsche, *On the Genealogy of Morals and Ecce Homo* (New York: Random House, 2010).

4. Alan D. Schrift, *Nietzsche's French Legacy: A Genealogy of Poststructuralism* (London: Routledge, 1995), 33.

THE PROBLEM

KEY POINTS

- *Sexuality Vol. 1* challenged the way scholars thought about sex, sexuality, and power, and challenged common ideas about sexuality's role in nineteenth-century society.

- Foucault's text rejected the theoretical approach founded on the work of the nineteenth-century political philosopher Karl Marx* and the founder of psychoanalysis* Sigmund Freud* that dominated academic thought in his field in the 1960s and 1970s.

- *Sexuality Vol. 1* offered a new way of thinking about repression and power, arguing against the ideas of scholars such as the German American cultural critic Herbert Marcuse,* and claiming that power cannot be located in one single place or person.

Core Question

Michel Foucault's *The History of Sexuality Vol. 1: The Will to Knowledge* challenged the way sexuality was understood both within the intellectual circles of his time, and by the public at large. The book's core question is: "Why does a society like ours speak so openly about sexual repression?" The way Foucault approached it was highly original. He developed an entirely new way of thinking about sexuality and power that went against current scholarship.

Sexuality Vol. 1 sought to demonstrate that sexuality is not simply something that the dominant classes (that is, the rich and powerful) of a society look to repress in the lower classes— a view held by many humanities* and social science* scholars during the 1960s and 1970s. Foucault disputes what he calls this "repressive hypothesis."* The repressive hypothesis assumes that power, whether in the form of law or of bourgeois* (middle-class) society, in general represses sexuality. For instance, it is considered improper to talk about sex openly, and it is assumed that only the lower classes satisfy their sexual appetites without restraint. In this sense, sexual liberation will come only if we radically break free from all these restrictions on sexuality. According to these views, power works solely in negative terms: it represses and prohibits instinctive sexual drives.

Foucault rejected this position. He argued instead that power is also positive and productive in the sense that it shapes the way we see the world, including our desires and preferences.

The text challenged the social movements of the 1960s and 1970s that, following the repressive hypothesis, claimed they were liberating the public from repressive attitudes left over from the nineteenth century. By maintaining that nineteenth-century views on sexuality were in fact more complex than scholars thought, Foucault suggested that the arguments of left-wing activists were overly simple and historically inaccurate.

> "[Modernity* made] the flesh into the root of all evil, shifting the most important moment of transgression from the act itself to the stirrings—so difficult to perceive and formulate—of desire. For this was an evil that afflicted the whole man, and in the most secret of forms."
>
> ——Michel Foucault, *The History of Sexuality Vol. 1: The Will to Knowledge*

The Participants

Foucault's text was partly a critique of Freudo-Marxism,* an approach to cultural analysis drawing on Sigmund Freud's psychoanalysis and Karl Marx's critique of the social and economic system of capitalism.* Freudian psychoanalysis sees culture as a product of people's actions and of our unconscious desires and suppressed urges. Marxist criticism sees culture in terms of the conflicts between people of different socioeconomic classes.

Viewed through the lens of Freudo-Marxism, sexuality is, above all, a tool for oppression. The upper classes of society decide what is proper and then use these rules to dominate the lower classes, while individuals face the conflict between their inner desires and society's ideas of what is acceptable. This idea can be attributed to the German psychoanalyst Wilhelm Reich.* In his theory of "sexual repression" Reich suggests that repression is a necessary part of capitalist exploitation. He argues that "the compulsion to control one's sexuality ... leads to the development of pathologic [diseased], emotionally tinged notions of honor and duty, bravery and self-control."[1] In Reich's view, repression could even make the masses ready to accept authoritarian forms of rule—systems in which personal liberty is sacrificed to governmental authority.

Foucault questioned Reich's views, but was especially interested in Reich's urge to speak about sexual repression. For Foucault, the efforts of psychiatrists and biologists to put sexuality into words showed their own biases. Toward the end of *Sexuality*

Vol. 1 he notes, "The fact that so many things were able to change in the sexual behavior of Western societies [the loosening of attitudes toward sex, aided by the widespread availability of the 'pill' and other birth-control methods, for example] without any of the promises or political conditions predicted by Reich being realized is sufficient proof that this whole sexual 'revolution,' this whole 'anti-repressive' struggle, represented nothing more, but nothing less—and its importance is undeniable—than a tactical shift and reversal in the great deployment of sexuality."[2]

By this, Foucault meant that although the sexual revolution was undeniably important, it was important for different reasons from those given to it by the political left. He saw it as a fascinating example of how different interest groups (scientific institutions, political parties, and so on) developed ideas about sex to further their own aims. Where "the great deployment of sexuality" in the Victorian era served to diagnose mental illnesses and restrict behavior, in the 1960s it became a means to take down these restrictions. For Foucault, the interesting thing is the consistency with which different institutions, with often opposing views, have used sexuality—that is, the discussion of sex—to advance their political agenda.

Foucault saw Reich as one of the strongest promoters of the repressive hypothesis and was very skeptical of the whole idea of sexual or other liberation. Foucault took a position against the Freudo-Marxist approaches that largely shaped the intellectual debates of his time and presented new ideas to replace those he was critiquing. His text set out to show how people in the nineteenth century *actually* thought about sex and sexuality, and, more broadly, to prove that power does not work the way many assume.

The Contemporary Debate

Sexuality Vol. 1 can also be seen to target the American-based German philosopher Herbert Marcuse. Although Marcuse's name is not directly mentioned anywhere in the text, Foucault often mentioned him in interviews in which he discussed his "repressive hypothesis." For example, in an interview he gave a year before *Sexuality Vol. 1* was published, Foucault distanced himself "from para-Marxists like Marcuse who give the notion of repression an exaggerated role."[3]

In the book itself, Foucault's rejection of Marcuse's ideas is clear when he talks about power. One of Marcuse's central and most influential ideas was the concept of the "great refusal."* He defined this as "the protest against unnecessary repression, the struggle for the ultimate form of freedom—'to live without anxiety'."[4] In other words, to live freely one must reject all forms of repression, and oppose the efforts of those in power to dictate how one should behave or what one should believe.

In contrast to Marcuse, Foucault claims that power does not reside in a single person or place, whose influence one can resist. Instead, power is multidimensional, distributed across relations and networks. As he puts it in *Sexuality Vol.1*, "there is no single locus of great Refusal, no soul of revolt, source of all rebellions, or pure law of the revolutionary."[5] This statement clearly suggests a critique of Marcuse's idea. Because power is spread out, rejecting power is much more complicated than Marcuse's theory suggests, for it involves countering more than the authority of a single person (a king, one's boss) or institution (the government, a company).

---

1. Wilhelm Reich, The Mass Psychology of Fascism, (New York: Farrar, Straus & Giroux, 1970), 54.

2. Michel Foucault, *The History of Sexuality Vol. 1: The Will to Knowledge,* trans. Robert Hurley (London: Penguin Books, 1998), 131.

3. Michel Foucault, *Power/Knowledge: Selected Interviews and Other Writings, 1972–1977,* ed. Colin Gordon, trans. Colin Gordon et al. (New York: Random House, Inc., 1980), 59.

4. Herbert Marcuse, *Eros and Civilization: A Philosophical Inquiry into Freud*, (Beacon Press, 1974 [1955]), 149–50.

5. Foucault, *Sexuality Vol. 1*, 95–6.

MODULE 4
THE AUTHOR'S CONTRIBUTION

KEY POINTS

- Foucault put forward an original theory of power as both dispersed and productive—having the capacity to *construct* desires, identities, and pleasures, rather than just repress them.

- He focused on the body, and not the individual, as the place where control over people is exercised.

- *Sexuality Vol. 1* was intended to be the first of six volumes that would analyze sexuality's role throughout the ages; *Vol. 1* looked at the nineteenth century, *Vol. 2** examined sexuality in ancient Greece, and *Vol. 3** considered ancient Rome.

Author's Aims

Michel Foucault's *The History of Sexuality Vol. 1: The Will to Knowledge* aimed to achieve three goals: to challenge the "repressive hypothesis,"* to show that sex from the late seventeenth century onwards was examined as an object of scientific analysis, and to advance a new theory about how power operates.

Foucault sought to show that experts such as psychologists,* biologists,* medical doctors, demographers* (those analyzing the ways in which a certain society is made up statistically) from the late seventeenth century onwards viewed sex as a problem of "truth"—a matter to be examined, written about, and understood. Related to this, he aimed to demonstrate that the modern view of eighteenth- and nineteenth-century bourgeois* society as repressive was part of the same dominant narrative that had sought to first repress sexuality. Put differently, he argued that this "knowledge" of a sexually repressive history was, itself, constructed: "Why do we say, with so much passion and so much resentment against our most recent past, against our present, and against ourselves, that we are repressed?"[1]

Foucault put forward an original theory of power as something dispersed, rather than located in any one person or place. By exploring how nineteenth-century thinkers studied sex, Foucault aimed to show that power is not only repressive, it is also productive, and has the capacity to *construct* desires, identities, and pleasures rather than just repress them. In short, Foucault set out to define "the regime of power-knowledge-pleasure that sustains the discourse on human sexuality in our part of the world."[2]

> *"Sexuality must not be thought of as a kind of natural given which power tries to hold in check, or as an obscure domain which knowledge tries gradually to uncover. It is the name that can be given to a historical construct."*
>
> —— Michel Foucault, *The History of Sexuality Vol. 1: The Will to Knowledge*

Approach

Foucault intended *Sexuality Vol. 1* to be the first of a six-volume work that would examine how sexuality was represented, and the role it played, throughout history. In *Vol. 1*, Foucault examines, compares, and contrasts theological,* psychiatric,* and medical texts and practices from the Middle Ages* to the nineteenth century in order to understand how views on sexuality changed in the eighteenth and nineteenth centuries.

Foucault approaches his analysis of the theoretical and practical context of sexuality by focusing on the body as the location of control over individuals. This focus on the body, instead of on the individual, is significant. The individual is not a basic, stable entity that those in power can target. Foucault wants to avoid focusing on any particular party in power relations. He emphasizes that it is not just institutions that oppress people, but that the most commonplace relations also influence institutions. That is, there is no main agent—active force—exercising power. Power, Foucault says, works bottom up as much as top down.

Contribution in Context

Because Foucault died from an HIV*-related illness shortly after the publication of *Vols. 2* and *3*, it is difficult to say how close he came to achieving his original aims. It is similarly impossible to know how our opinion of his work, and our approach to his entire output, would be different had all six volumes of *The History of Sexuality* been completed. The delay in the publication of *Vols. 2* and *3* (they appeared eight years after the first volume) can be read as evidence that he lost interest in the project, or that he reached some sort of intellectual stalemate. However, Foucault's delay can also point to troubles he had with his publishers.[3] Although Foucault's initial aim for the project has only been partly realized, the volumes he managed to publish clearly changed the way scholars thought about sex. They also contributed to the discussion of power relations and knowledge initiated by his earlier works.

Although the books share some of the same concerns—notably the relationship between sexuality and power, the regulation of desire, and the socially constructed nature of the body—*Vol. 2* and *Vol. 3* of *The History of Sexuality* take a rather different approach to *Vol. 1*. In *Vol. 2*, Foucault considers the role of erotic pleasure across ancient Greek culture, focusing on its depiction in numerous ancient Greek texts. In *Vol. 3*, he examines sexuality's role in ancient Rome, focusing on the meditations on sex by philosophers such as Seneca,* Plutarch* and Epictetus* to understand how views of sex changed over the course of the Roman Empire. Both volumes seek to understand the reasons behind Western culture's tendency to judge sexuality in moral terms, and to regulate it far more than other physical appetites such as hunger, sleep, or aggression.

---

1. Michel Foucault, *The History of Sexuality Vol. 1: The Will to Knowledge,* trans. Robert Hurley (London: Penguin Books, 1998), 8–9.

2. Foucault, *Sexuality Vol. 1,* 11.

3. See Daniel Defert, "Chronology," in *A Companion to Foucault*, eds. Christopher Falzon et al. (Chichester: Wiley & Sons, 2013), 60.

SECTION 2
IDEAS

MAIN IDEAS

KEY POINTS

* *Sexuality Vol. 1* examines the blossoming of ideas around sex in Western societies since the eighteenth century.

* The text challenges common ideas about nineteenth-century views of sex and sexuality. Foucault goes on to examine the scientific study of sexuality from the same period, to show how knowledge is constructed, and power can be productive.

* Although Foucault's writing style can make the text difficult to follow, it is helped by the way he frequently anticipates and answers the reader's questions.

Key Themes

Michel Foucault's *The History of Sexuality Vol. 1: The Will to Knowledge* explores how various ideas about sex and new ways of talking about it have developed and spread in modern Western societies since the eighteenth century. The text challenges the "repressive hypothesis,"* which claimed that the dominant classes of society (the wealthy middle classes and the Church) emphasized the reproductive function of sex, while suppressing and silencing its pleasurable qualities. Sex in Western societies came to be restricted and was considered acceptable only in the private space of the married heterosexual* couple's bedroom. According to this premise, even the discussion of sex was suppressed in nineteenth-century society.

Foucault asks important questions—one historical, a second theoretical, and a third historical-political—about the repressive hypothesis. First, he asks whether sexual repression was a historical fact: Did it actually happen? Second, he asks whether power in our society works through repression. Third, he asks whether the concept of sexual liberation is part of the same network of power that it so forcefully denounces, misnaming it as "repression."

Foucault proposes that the call for sexual liberation in the West at the time he was working on the book in fact parallels the history of repression that the liberators wished to oppose. Foucault proposes that, instead of simply repressing sex, the more powerful classes had actually sought to make people talk about it, and to make it an object of scientific analysis. The themes of *Sexuality Vol. 1* are: the relationship between the scientific study of sex and the state's regulation of sexual behavior; the evolution of sex and sexuality as concepts; the role that modern scientific disciplines have played in shaping our understanding of sexuality; and, finally, the relationship between sex, power, and knowledge.

> "The society that emerged in the nineteenth century—bourgeois, capitalist, or industrial society, call it what you will—did not confront sex with a fundamental refusal of recognition. On the contrary, it put into operation an entire machinery for producing true discourses concerning it."
>
> —— Michel Foucault, *The History of Sexuality Vol. 1: The Will to Knowledge*

Exploring the Ideas

The most important argument Foucault sets out in *Sexuality Vol. 1* has to do with the relationship between knowledge (in this case, from the study of sexuality), power, and the construction of identity. Foucault challenges the popular view that sexuality has been clearly repressed since the start of bourgeois* society. Instead, he claims that sexuality in the eighteenth and nineteenth centuries became an object of scientific analysis within the budding fields of biology,* demography,* pedagogy,* and psychiatry.* These disciplines produced knowledge about sexual desires, orientations, and preferences that were supposed to be linked to the truth about someone's character. Foucault calls this *scientia sexualis*—the science of sex.

One of the effects of *scientia sexualis*, Foucault argues, is that nineteenth-century society came to view sexuality as deeply connected to a person's identity. In other words, sexuality was viewed as indicating an individual's true self. Scientists began to study people they thought exhibited "abnormal" sexual desires or behavior. The sexuality of the mentally ill, criminals, and sex between people of the same gender whipped up scientists' curiosity. The knowledge scientists gained from their studies led to the creation of distinct categories of individuals based on their sexual preferences.

According to Foucault, the term "homosexual"* was a product of one such study. The term first entered scientific discussion in 1870 through an article by the German neurologist* and psychiatrist Carl Westphal,* who used it to define a particular type of person with a particular kind of character—or as Foucault calls it, "a hermaphrodism* (having both male and female organs) of the soul."[1] Westphal looked at the act of sex between two men and built an entire theory, and identity category, around it. Such categorizations, like *scientia sexualis* as a whole, in turn gave rise to new forms of regulation designed to curb "abnormal" sexual behavior.[2]

Foucault concludes from this that power in the modern period does not operate primarily through direct repression (for instance, stopping people from talking about their sexual fantasies). Instead, power operates through the production of knowledge (gathering detailed information about people's fantasies, and then using that information to develop theories about what makes up normal and abnormal behavior, and laws to uphold those principles). Foucault concludes that a society's knowledge producers (the institutions that analyze human behavior, draw conclusions, and then feed that information back into society) play a central role in influencing its desires and ideals. It is in this sense that Foucault argues power is productive. The idea that our sexual behavior (and for Foucault, our behavior in general) is an effect of the power structures in our societies is among Foucault's most important contributions to the social sciences.[*]

Language and Expression

The unclear phrasing and complex arguments of *Sexuality Vol. 1* might lead a reader to believe it was aimed at an academic audience, but Foucault intended to intervene in the public debate as much as in academic discussions.

Foucault's efforts to speak to an audience beyond academia

can be seen as part of a broader shift in his intellectual thought. For historian François Dosse, the clearest difference between Foucault's work in the 1970s and that of the previous decade is his personal involvement in grassroots activism, especially in the *Groupe d'Information sur les Prisons* (Prison Information Group*), an organization in France fighting for inmates' rights. Dosse argues that the most important "shift in Foucault's position" in the 1970s was to become "personally involved in his theoretical object of study."[3]

This shift, however, is not reflected in Foucault's writing style, which does little to help average readers understand its content. As Foucault himself admitted, his arguments tend to roll out "at the cost of a certain difficulty for the author and the reader."[4] Readers new to Foucault will notice that his work assumes that his audience is familiar with a broad range of cultural phenomena. His arguments are often peppered with hard-to-understand references, while his paragraph-long sentences can make it difficult for even an experienced academic to understand what he is saying. Readers might take comfort, however, in the fact that *Sexuality Vol. 1* is an easy read compared to earlier works of Foucault's, such as *The Birth of the Clinic** (1963) and *The Order of Things** (1966).

Another feature of Foucault's style worth noting is his tendency to advance his arguments by first questioning them. This rhetorical method allows him to construct a text that anticipates and answers the reader's questions—making the work somewhat easier to navigate.

1. Michel Foucault, *The History of Sexuality Vol. 1: The Will to Knowledge,* trans. Robert Hurley (London: Penguin Books, 1998), 43.

2. Foucault, *Sexuality Vol. 1,* 45.

3. See Francois Dosse, *History of Structuralism. Volume II. The Sign Sets 1967–Present,* trans. Deborah Glassman (Minneapolis: University of Minnesota Press, 1998), 249.

4. See Paul Rabinow, "Series Preface" in *Michel Foucault: Ethics, Subjectivity and Truth*, ed. Paul Rabinow (New York: The New Press, 1997), vii.

SECONDARY IDEAS

KEY POINTS

* Foucault's *Sexuality Vol. 1* considers the workings of power, and advances the idea that our very identities are, at least in part, shaped by those who produce knowledge—meaning that even those who resist authority must do so from within the system they are opposing.

* This concept has been questioned and to an extent misunderstood by the academic community, which has led to significant controversies.

* Foucault's fertile work has prompted a huge amount of intellectual debate and academic articles; more recently, the book has been criticized for its failure to consider the role of colonial oppression and racism in the history he examines ("colonialism"* is the policy of settling and exploiting a foreign territory and its people).

Other Ideas

The most important secondary idea in Michel Foucault's *The History of Sexuality Vol. 1: The Will to Knowledge* is his understanding of power as dispersed, or spread out. While his discussion of power might appear secondary, simply supporting his general aim of explaining the constructed nature of sexual categories, it is in fact crucial to understanding the full complexity of his work.

These ideas occupy a central position and are presented clearly in the last chapters, "The Deployment of Sexuality" and "Right of

Death and Power over Life." Here, Foucault extends his discussion of sexuality to propose a new theory of power, criticizing the view that power acts in a one-way manner, from top to bottom. Instead, he argues, power is a complex force that enables desires, pleasures, and identities.

Foucault's idea of power as dispersed seeks to explain how power operates and how resistance to power might take place. This proposition was influential in the development both of political activism and of certain principles of post-Marxism* (theoretical approaches grounded in Marxist* theory but extending, reversing, or modifying it) and anarchist political theory* (theory founded on the principle that the institution of hierarchical government is illegitimate). However, Foucault's arguments on power were not without their critics, and the discussions that they set off are instructive.

In the final section, "Right of Death and Power over Life," Foucault reviews the difference between the exercise of power in earlier times and its exercise in modern societies. In earlier times, power acted in a "deductive" way; the ruler would exert his authority by taking his or her subjects' taxes, wealth, land, and life. In modern societies, power is "productive," being used to produce a certain kind of individual through sophisticated methods of regulation and control. Withholding or granting birth control, banning or granting abortion, championing heterosexuality,* and recommending a certain number of children per family are all methods involving the regulation of sexual and reproductive behavior. Modern society uses these means to control the population and ensure citizens follow a certain way of life. In this sense, sex in modern societies is seen as a practice to be administered.

> "Power comes from below; that is, there is no binary and all-encompassing opposition between rulers and ruled at the root of power relations, and serving as a general matrix."
>
> —— Michel Foucault, *The History of Sexuality Vol. 1: The Will to Knowledge*

Exploring the Ideas

In *Sexuality Vol. 1* Foucault argues that the ways we think about our sexuality and the sexuality of people around us are closely related to the sexual categories produced by modern scientific institutions. The scientific community has great power over how we perceive human behavior and desire and, in turn, ourselves. When scientists tell us something is unhealthy or unnatural, we believe them. To the extent that we do not question these ideas but take them to be facts, we are already, unknowingly within subject-to-power relations—roughly, the exercise of hierarchical power. Resistance, the effort to rebel against authority, is no different; it takes place within power relations, and cannot be exercised from an external point.

This crucial idea has, however, led to misunderstandings. Foucault has often been misinterpreted as arguing that, since power is everywhere, there is no escape from it and, therefore, resistance is futile.[1] In fact, Foucault argues the opposite. The point of his argument is to challenge the idea that there is one power that we have to oppose. In his words, there is "no binary and all-encompassing opposition between rulers and ruled."[2] Moreover,"Where there is power, there is resistance and yet, or rather consequently, this resistance is never in a position of exteriority in relation to power."[3]

What Foucault meant by this is that any form of resistance has to recognize that it is already involved in power relations. Resistance is not futile; the point is that those who resist must also recognize that they are not doing so from some pure position freed from power. American queer* studies scholar David Halperin* clarifies the kind of power Foucault is talking about, observing that "some of Foucault's critics on the Left may simply have misunderstood his claim, 'power is everywhere' ... When he says that 'power is everywhere,' Foucault is not talking about power in the sense of coercive and irresistible force ... rather, he is referring to what might be called *liberal* power*—that is, to the kind of power ... which takes as its objects 'free subjects' and defines itself wholly in relation to them and to their freedom."[4]

Institutions, in other words, have exerted authority by regulating how sex is talked about, and what sexual behaviors or preferences a society deems "healthy" or "unhealthy." But these social codes have, in turn, gained a life of their own (so to speak), shaping views and behaviors in ways rulers could not have foreseen. Power and sexuality are linked in modernity* because, in this era, sexuality is regulated both directly (through rules) and indirectly (through social codes that cannot be said to come from any one specific source).

Overlooked

Sexuality Vol. 1 has provoked a rich intellectual debate, and has been followed by a considerable number of academic texts discussing the various points it raises. Scholars have questioned some of the work's ideas, including the text's Eurocentrism*— that is, the extent to which its arguments are limited to European culture, and neglect to consider the sexuality or viewpoint of other races and ethnic groups (including people who still lived under European colonial rule, or were just gaining independence, at the time Foucault was writing).

In 1988, only 12 years after the book's original publication, the Eurocentricity of Foucault's thought became the subject of debate. In *The Predicament of Culture* (1988), the American anthropologist James Clifford* warned that the "scrupulously ethnocentric" nature of Foucault's approach "has avoided all comparative appeals to other worlds of meaning."[5] Similar objections have come from the field of postcolonial* studies (inquiry into the various cultural and social legacies of colonialism). The scholar Gayatri Chakravorty Spivak,* for example, in her famous essay "Can the Subaltern Speak?", positioned Foucault within a Western literary tradition that denies voice and agency (the power to act) to non-Western populations.

It was not until 1995, with the US anthropologist* Ann Stoler's* *Race and the Education of Desire: Foucault's History of Sexuality and the Colonial Order of Things* (1995), that a fertile discussion and radical rereading of Foucault from a postcolonial angle truly began. Stoler argued that Foucault ignores how Western modernity was shaped to a large extent through its interaction with non-European populations and, more importantly, through racism, colonialism and slavery. While sympathetic to Foucault's ideas, Stoler maintained that Foucault presents a history of European sexuality that fails to see the ways that European middle-class identity was largely formed in opposition to colonized cultures. "Why for Foucault," she asked forcefully, "do colonial bodies never figure as a possible site of the articulation of nineteenth-century European sexuality?"[6]

By rethinking the history of sexuality based on the unequal power between European colonizers and the colonized (in Africa, Asia, and Oceania), the book brought to light a largely neglected side of Foucault's text: that of race in relation to the way bourgeois* people grew to see themselves. Without abandoning Foucault's overall aim of disturbing stereotypical ideas of sexual identities, Stoler's text offered a productive, culturally specific critique of *Sexuality Vol. 1*, and opened up new ways of using Foucault's ideas in the study of colonial rule.[7]

---

1. David Halperin, *Saint Foucault: Towards a Gay Hagiography* (New York: Oxford University Press, 1995), 18.

2. Michel Foucault, *The History of Sexuality Vol. 1: The Will to Knowledge,* trans. Robert Hurley (London: Penguin Books, 1998), 94.

3. Foucault, *Sexuality Vol. 1*, 95.

4. Halperin, *Saint Foucault*, 18.

5. James Clifford, *The Predicament of Culture: Twentieth-Century Ethnography, Literature, and Art* (Cambridge, Mass: Harvard University Press, 1988), 264–5.

6. See Ann Laura Stoler, *Race and the Education of Desire: Foucault's History of Sexuality and the Colonial Order of Things* (Durham, North Carolina: Duke University Press, 1995), i.

7. Stoler, *Race and the Education of Desire*, 1–2.

MODULE 7
ACHIEVEMENT

KEY POINTS

- Foucault's novel approach introduced a new way of thinking about sexuality, the production of knowledge, and the workings of power that have since influenced various fields across the humanities* and social sciences.*

- The first publication of *Sexuality Vol. 1* in 1976, and its 1978 English translation, had a great impact on homosexual* and queer* activists—activists who wish to challenge widely held assumptions regarding sexuality and gender* identity with the aim of reshaping structures of power and the balance of equality.

- Although recognized as a groundbreaking work, the book has also been criticized by feminist* and postcolonial* scholars who viewed it as androcentric* (focusing on the male experience) and Eurocentric.*

Assessing the Argument

Michel Foucault's *The History of Sexuality Vol. 1: The Will to Knowledge* is highly original in the way it opposes the Freudo-Marxist* analysis of sexuality then dominant in intellectual circles. Instead, Foucault proposes that sex is a set of ideas constructed by society and shaped in and by scientific institutions, and that these ideas are used to regulate individuals and populations. Foucault makes this argument through a complex historical and theoretical analysis that traces the rise, at the end of the seventeenth century, of a new discipline that viewed sex as an object of scientific study.

This new approach informed the way people were labeled as normal or abnormal.

Foucault's approach gave birth to a whole genre of studies around sexuality. These studies, which expanded substantially during the 1990s and now hold a leading place in scholarly debates, regard sexuality as an effect of power and not necessarily in strict opposition to it.

This latter point relates to another original idea that set the text apart from similar studies: Foucault's understanding of power. He made the significant claim that power does not only work in negative ways—it does not, for example, serve simply to prohibit or repress instinctual drives (such as the "sex drive") that desire unimpeded expression. Nor does power work only in a simple top-down direction. For Foucault, power is also productive in the sense that it creates preferences, orientations, and desires in people.

This idea of power not as a total force but, rather, as a set of relations proved key for the development of post-Marxist* political theory. Foucault's work has been central for post-Marxists, such as the Argentinian political-theorist Ernesto Laclau,* the Belgian political-theorist Chantal Mouffe,* and the Italian philosopher Antonio Negri.*

> "Pleasure and power do not cancel or turn back against one another; they seek out, overlap, and reinforce one another. They are linked together by complex mechanisms and devices of excitation and excitement."
>
> ——Michel Foucault, *The History of Sexuality Vol 1: The Will to Knowledge*

Achievement in Context

Although the title of Foucault's work indicates that it is a history of sexuality, it would be simplistic to see it only as a historical text in the conventional sense. Foucault never thought of himself as a professional historian; instead he sought to expose the basic assumptions in our understanding of modern Western societies. As such, the work must also be seen as an examination of how concepts such as truth, knowledge, and power relate to the way sexual practices are represented and understood.

By challenging these positions, Foucault's work offered new ways of thinking about sexuality—seeing it as an effect of social conditions and not as pure instinct. Furthermore, Foucault's idea of "power" as multiple arrangements of relations and forces, and not just the use or threat of force by a ruler, has had a long-lasting influence in the intellectual world.

Foucault's text was also groundbreaking outside of academia. Following first publication in 1976 and its English translation two years later, the book had a significant impact on gay and queer activists during the 1980s and 1990s. Professor David Halperin, a scholar noted for his contribution to queer theory, has observed that when gay activists in New York during the late 1980s were asked about their influences, they would give "without the slightest hesitation or a single exception, the following answer: Michel Foucault, *The History of Sexuality Volume I.*"[1]

Limitations

Although the claims that Foucault makes are truly pioneering, due to the book's short length they are not always analyzed in depth. In this sense, the text as a whole seems to be a promise of something more that will follow. This makes sense as *Sexuality Vol. 1* was intended to be the first of a six-volume work. It is also worth noting that the text is not as thorough and rigorous as one might expect to find in a historical study—a point that has been seen as a serious weakness.[2]

Among the book's most frequently cited limitations is that it focuses almost exclusively on the role of sexuality in Western modernity.* One might counter this claim, however, by arguing that the object of Foucault's study, "modernity,"* refers not only to a historical period of the Western world, but to a set of practices, approaches to knowledge, and institutions that have spread globally. For example, the discussion of sexuality based on scientific knowledge that has (now, or in the past) labeled certain practices as "perversions" or "pathological" has by now extended to other parts of the world. *Sexuality Vol. 1,* in other words, arrives at conclusions that can be analyzed in relation to non-European societies and populations.

Other criticisms of the text are harder to dismiss. For instance, Foucault's only mention of sexuality in civilizations other than in current, or ancient, Europe occurs in Part Three, "Scientia Sexualis,"* where he contrasts what he calls the "two great procedures for producing the truth of sex."[3] Here he argues that in China, Japan, India, Rome, and the Arab-Muslim world truth about sex has been understood by means of *ars erotica*,* that is to say from teachings about pleasure and experience itself. This is in contrast to modern Western societies, where truth about sex is informed by scientia sexualis, a means of understanding sexuality based on the production of knowledge about it, such as scientific study or the ritual of confession.* This analysis has sparked criticism from scholars such as the Tunisian sociologist Fathi Triki,* who has termed it both naïve and inaccurate.[4]

Sexuality Vol. 1 has also been criticized by feminist critics for its "blindness to sexual violence"[5] and for being androcentric— that is, for focusing on the experience of men.[6] The most frequently censured part of the text is Foucault's account of a case in 1867, when a farmer from the town of Lapcourt, France, was turned over to the authorities for having "obtained a few caresses from a little girl."[7] For Foucault the remarkable thing in the story is that, as a result of his act, the man became the object of "a judicial action, a medical intervention, a careful clinical examination, and an entire theoretical elaboration."[8] For Foucault, the way the man was turned into a "pure object of medicine and knowledge"[9] indicates how, through the use of legal-psychiatric categories, sexual acts in modern times came to be seen as revealing a person's inner self (in this case, a man capable of sexual harassment or rape). Feminist writers have criticized this interpretation for ignoring the victim and the violence she suffered, and focusing only on the point of view of the man accused of committing the act.[10]

1. See David Halperin, *Saint Foucault: Towards a Gay Hagiography* (New York: Oxford University Press, 1995), 16.

2. See, for example, Jeremy R. Carrette, *Foucault and Religion: Spiritual Corporality and Political Spirituality* (London: Routledge, 2000), 131; Elizabeth A. Clark, "Foucault, The Fathers and Sex," *Journal of the American Academy of Religion* 56, no .4 (1988): 625.

3. Michel Foucault, *The History of Sexuality Vol. 1: The Will to Knowledge,* trans. Robert Hurley (London: Penguin Books, 1998), 57.

4. Janet Afary and Kevin B. Anderson, "Foucault, Gender and Male Homosexualities in Mediterranean and Muslim Society," in *Foucault and the Iranian Revolution: Gender and the Seductions of Islamism* (Chicago: University of Chicago Press, 2005), 138–62, citation on 141.

5. Kelly H. Ball, "'More or Less Raped': Foucault, Causality, and Feminist Critiques of Sexual Violence," *philoSOPHIA* 3, no.1 (2013): 53.

6. Kate Soper, "Productive Contradictions," in *Up Against Foucault: Explorations of Some Tensions Between Foucault and Feminism*, ed. Caroline Ramazanoglu (New York: Routledge), 29.

7. Foucault, *Sexuality Vol. 1*, 31.

8. Foucault, *Sexuality Vol. 1*, 31.

9. Foucault, *Sexuality Vol. 1*, 31.

10. For a discussion see Ball, "'More or Less Raped'."

MODULE 8
PLACE IN THE AUTHOR'S WORK

KEY POINTS

- Published in 1976, *Sexuality Vol. 1* is among Foucault's last works, and marks an important moment in the evolution of his thought.

- As with Foucault's other books, *Sexuality Vol. 1* is concerned with power and knowledge and the construction of identity, but it approaches these in a new way, through the concepts of "governmentality"* (practices of governing that aim to shape citizens' conduct instead of openly suppressing them) and "biopower"* (a term Foucault uses for an "explosion" of techniques used to subjugate individual bodies and entire populations).

- Foucault's influence on the development of the fields of queer* theory and gender* and sexuality* studies is undisputed; together with his *Discipline and Punish,* * the three volumes of *The History of Sexuality* are his most well-known and most frequently cited books.

Positioning

Michel Foucault's *The History of Sexuality Vol. 1: The Will to Knowledge* examines the subject of sexuality. But his views on the workings of power can be traced to earlier texts. The most obvious is *Discipline and Punish*, dealing with prisons, which he published a year earlier, in 1975. Foucault regarded *Sexuality Vol. 1* as a continuation of this earlier book.[1]

In *Discipline and Punish*, Foucault discussed changes in the

Western penal system (especially prisons) during the eighteenth and nineteenth centuries. He argued persuasively that, around that time, the physical abuse of offenders gradually gave way to punishment based on analyzing the criminal for reasons why he or she committed offences, and advancing scientific research into the so-called "criminal mind." Such research was also used to determine whether the criminal could be reformed, made "normal," and reintegrated into society. Rather than sentencing an offender to death, doctors would seek to eradicate the bad behavior. During that time, "a corpus [body] of knowledge, techniques, 'scientific' discourses is formed and becomes entangled with the practice of the power to punish."[2] Traces of these ideas are evident in *Sexuality Vol.* 1, which is also concerned with how knowledge is used to produce new forms of regulation and control.

According to scholars such as Alan D. Schrift,* Foucault's writing career can be divided into three separate periods: an earlier "archaeological" phase, during which he was focused on questions of discourse and language ("archaeology" is the study of history through the physical remains of human activity and the analysis of objects); a second "genealogical"* phase focusing on the relation between power and knowledge; and a third "ethical" phase concerned with subjectivity* (here meaning the ways in which individual selfhood, or identity, develops).

For Schrift, the archaeological period included *Madness and Civilization** (1964), *The Order of Things** (1966), and *The Archaeology of Knowledge** (1969), which share a concern with "the relations of knowledge, language, truth." The genealogical period, which focuses specifically on power, includes *Discipline and Punish* (1975) and *The History of Sexuality Vol. 1 (*1976). The ethical period includes *The History of Sexuality Vols. 2** and *3** (1984), which stand out from Foucault's previous works in their focus on the "construction of the ethical/sexual subject or self."[3] However, these categories are in no way final, and they have often been contested as overly simplistic. Foucault himself would likely have resisted such labeling since he was skeptical about fixed categories, and because of his fascination with the motives of scholars when they insisted on making them.

> *"The omnipresence of power: not because it has the privilege of consolidating everything under its invincible unity, but because it is produced from one moment to the next, at every point, or rather in every relation from one point to another. Power is everywhere; not because it embraces everything, but because it comes from everywhere."*
>
> —— Michel Foucault, *The History of Sexuality Vol. 1: The Will to Knowledge*

Integration

The most important of Foucault's ideas appears in a complex discussion he sets out halfway through *Sexuality Vol. 1*, regarding the ways power operates in modern societies.

According to Foucault, power—and, specifically, *modern* power—does not operate from top to bottom, as "there is no binary and all-encompassing opposition between rulers and ruled."[4] As such, there is no single and totalitarian "power" that represses and prohibits desires: there are power relations that are aided and strengthened by different techniques that aim to control, as he describes it, "men's existence, men as living bodies."[5]

Foucault introduces the term "biopower" to refer to this idea, which is one of the most important concepts in his later work. In particular, biopower relates to another concept of Foucault: "governmentality." He coined this term to define practices of governing that aim to shape citizens' conduct (their behavior as well as their thoughts), instead of openly suppressing them—for instance, the use of scientific knowledge about sex to regulate it.

Although Foucault's individual texts share many themes, they also express quite noticeable differences that reflect the evolution of his thinking. For instance, Foucault's early works, such as *Madness and Civilization* and *The Birth of the Clinic** (1963) were influenced by structuralist* thought, in contrast to his later works, which could be termed poststructuralist.*

Structuralism is a theoretical approach, according to which elements of culture become intelligible if studied in relation to the larger structures and systems in which they belong. Poststructuralism questions the existence of these structures—and, indeed, the belief that we can be entirely certain that objective knowledge is possible at all, given that it is impossible to escape the cultural assumptions with which we begin any analysis.

In *The Archaeology of Knowledge*, Foucault describes his early works as a "very imperfect sketch,"[6] finding it "mortifying ... that [his] analyses were conducted in terms of cultural totality."[7]

This quote illustrates the difference not only between Foucault's early and late works, but the difference between structuralism and poststructuralism.

Structuralist thought seeks to understand a particular element of culture through the society's structures of which it is a part. So, for instance, in *The Birth of the Clinic* Foucault traces the development of the medical profession as a whole through a history of the medical clinic, in order to consider how knowledge of the human body and human health is produced by what he calls the "medical gaze."* A poststructuralist, by contrast, would not claim to be able to understand the subject in its entirety, admitting instead that, as a participant in the study, he or she could not help but be biased. In other words, in his later writings Foucault is aware that he himself is writing from within an institution, as a professor in twentieth-century France, and that this limits the scope of what he can understand.

Significance

Although scholarly discussions of sexuality have shifted since the book was written, *Sexuality Vol. 1* remains one of the key and most quoted texts in the fields of queer theory and gender and sexuality studies. Queer theory is an approach to cultural analysis that begins by acknowledging the instability and uncertainty of sexual identity and of knowledge itself; sexuality studies is inquiry into the ways in which sexuality (roughly, our preferences and orientations) is constructed and understood.

Since it was first published, the theory that Foucault proposed in *Sexuality Vol. 1* has regularly been cited and treated as a point of reference by highly respected scholars across the world. According to the *Times Higher Education* magazine, Foucault was the most quoted author in the humanities* and social sciences* in 2007.[8]

Sexuality Vol. 1 can be seen to bring together and extend parts of Foucault's earlier thought. The text develops and voices more fully the relationship between power, knowledge, and the body that is central to all his work. If one were to state the aim of Foucault's academic career, it would perhaps be: to understand how power operates across societies and academic disciplines, to understand the relationship between power and knowledge, and to understand how the human body, human sexuality, and concepts such as madness, criminality, and surveillance have historically been used to observe citizens' behavior or alter it. *Sexuality Vol. 1* is an important step toward his goal.

---

1. See David Macey, *The Lives of Michel Foucault* (New York: Pantheon, 1993), 354.

2. Michel Foucault, *Discipline and Punish*, trans. Alan Sheridan (New York: Random House, 1977), 23.

3. See Alan D. Schrift, *Nietzsche's French Legacy: A Genealogy of Poststructuralism* (London: Routledge, 1995), 35–7.

4. Michel Foucault, *The History of Sexuality Vol. 1: The Will to Knowledge,* trans. Robert Hurley (London: Penguin Books, 1998), 98.

5. Foucault, *Sexuality Vol. 1,* 89.

6. Michel Foucault, *The Archaeology of Knowledge,* trans. A. M. Sheridan Smith (London: Tavistock Publications Limited, 1972), 15.

7. Foucault, *The Archaeology of Knowledge*, 15.

8. "Most Cited Authors of Books in the Humanities, 2007," *Times Higher Education*, accessed November 15, 2015, http://www.timeshighereducation.co.uk/405956.article.

SECTION 3
IMPACT

THE FIRST RESPONSES

KEY POINTS

- *The History of Sexuality Vol. 1* was received negatively by many scholars on publication; feminist critics debated about the book intensely, some welcoming Michel Foucault's questioning of sexual categories, others criticizing some of his views on sexual violence.

- While Foucault responded to a few of his critics in interviews, for the most part he did not engage with the debate.

- The shift in focus in the second and third volumes of *History of Sexuality* can however be interpreted as an effort on Foucault's part to take his critics' points on board.

Criticism

When it was first published, Michel Foucault's *The History of Sexuality Vol. 1: The Will to Knowledge* received a great deal of unfavorable attention.[1] In its first years the most serious criticism focused on particular aspects of the text rather than on the work as whole. While a lot of criticism came from a Marxist* and psychoanalytic* point of view, perhaps the most lasting and fertile early discussions of *Sexuality Vol. 1* emerged from a feminist* background.

The American academic and writer Biddy Martin* warned in 1982 of "the danger that Foucault's challenges to traditional categories, if taken to a 'logical' conclusion ... could make the question of women's oppression obsolete."[2] She further warned feminists "not [to] be seduced by the work of Foucault."[3] Although feminists were for the most part sympathetic to Foucault's method as well as to his belief in the constructed nature of sexual categories, writers like Martin pointed out the limitations of Foucault's work when it came to addressing their social demands toward equality between the sexes.

Other feminists criticized Foucault's ideas about sexual violence. The first article to raise the issue was "Our Costs and Their Benefits" (1978) by the French feminist scholar and activist Monique Plaza.* The article addressed Foucault's views on France's rape law that he voiced in 1977, a year after the publication of *Sexuality Vol. 1*, during a debate over amending the law. Extending some of the claims he made in *Sexuality Vol. 1*, Foucault claimed that cases of rape should be seen and punished by the law in the same way as all other acts of "violence"—a punch in the face, for example.[4] He argued that the attacker's "sexuality" should not be punished by the law.

Plaza's article, in which she accused Foucault of "de-sexualizing rape," looked to take apart Foucault's argument. According to Plaza, Foucault saw sexuality as an effect of a deployment (that is, the use) of power, of which women's bodies were the prime victims. Plaza claimed that by "not forbidding the deployment of power which has as its object of privileged appropriation the bodies of women"[5] (that is to say, by not forbidding the use of force to take control of women's bodies), Foucault ends up reproducing the same power structures that he has almost certainly opposed (in this case, the ways in which men have historically taken possession of female bodies). As two British commentators have written, "in seeking to rewrite the law on rape in such a way as to punish violence but decriminalise sexuality, he is defending men's existing right to possess women's bodies."[6]

> "The essential point is that sex was not only a matter of sensation and pleasure, of law and taboo, but also of truth and falsehood, that the truth of sex became something fundamental, useful, or dangerous, precious or formidable: in short, that sex was constituted as a problem of truth."
>
> —— Michel Foucault, *The History of Sexuality Vol. 1: The Will to Knowledge*

Responses

Because Foucault died in 1984, eight years after *Sexuality Vol. 1* was originally published in France and six years after its English translation, and most of the scholarly critiques on Foucault's work were written in the 1980s and 1990s, he did not have a chance to reply to most of them.

We have some responses to his first critics, however. In an interview a few years after the publication of *Sexuality Vol. 1*, Foucault responded to the feminist criticism that he had dismissed sexual violence and desexualized rape.[7] He stated: "I say 'freedom of sexual choice' and not 'freedom of sexual acts' because there are sexual acts like rape which should not be permitted."[8]

One of the most common accusations against Foucault is that, since he sees power as not being exclusively localized in government and the state but as exercised throughout the social body (the whole of society), resistance is impossible. However, in a later interview, he directly rejected this accusation, stating that "the claim that 'you see power everywhere, thus there is no room for freedom' seems to me absolutely inadequate. The idea that power is a system of domination that controls everything and leaves no room for freedom cannot be attributed to me."[9]

Conflict and Consensus

Foucault saw his work as necessarily subject to change, and although his books share many of the same themes, the differences between his earliest studies and his last show the extent to which he sought to develop and refine his ideas.

There is also evidence that some of the changes in his methodology and approach were as a result of criticisms of his earlier work. For instance, one might interpret his focus, in *Vol. 2** and *Vol. 3** of *The History of Sexuality*, on practices of resistance against certain social systems of power as a response to critics' claims that *Vol. 1* failed to fully address these. Foucault himself never directly commented on this—but the shift in tone between *Vol. 1* and the following two volumes is significant, and could well have been influenced by the criticism of the first volume. This shift also resulted in a far more sympathetic response from feminist critics to Foucault's later work on the "care of the self" in *Vol. 3*. For many, its discussion of the nature of sexual identity and its understanding of sexual behavior had an ethical dimension; the text offered a model for understanding individual identity in terms of our responsibilities to others.[10]

Finally, it is worth noting that for all the negative criticism it received at first, Foucault's *Sexuality Vol. 1* brought about a new understanding of how sexuality, desire, and institutional power relate to each other. While some of his ideas on specific issues such as rape remain controversial, his main ideas regarding the relationship between knowledge, power, and identity remain highly influential. Foucault himself continues to be among the most cited authors in the humanities* and social sciences,* and one of the most influential scholars since the 1970s.

---

1. Daniel Defert, "Chronology," in *A Companion to Foucault*, eds. Christopher Falzon et al. (Chichester: Wiley & Sons, 2013), 63.

2. Biddy Martin, "Feminism, Criticism, and Foucault," *New German Critique* 27 (1982): 17.

3. Martin, "Feminism, Criticism, and Foucault," 7.

4. Michel Foucault, "La Folie Encircle," cited in Dani Cavallaro, *French Feminist Theory: An Introduction* (London: Continuum, 2003), 102.

5. See Monique Plaza, "Our Costs and Their Benefits," in *Sex in Question: French Materialist Feminism*, eds. Diana Leonard and Lisa Adkins (London: Taylor & Francis, 1996), 185.

6. See Diana Leonard and Lisa Adkins, "Reconstructing French Feminism: Commodification, Materialism and Sex," in *Sex in Question*, 18.

7. See Monique Plaza, "Our Costs and Their Benefits," in *Sex in Question*, 185.

8. Michel Foucault, "Sexual Choice, Sexual Act," trans. James O'Higgins, in *Michel Foucault: Ethics, Subjectivity and Truth*, ed. Paul Rabinow (New York: The New Press, 1997), 143.

9. Michel Foucault, "The Ethics of the Concern for Self as a Practice of Freedom," trans. P. Aranaov and D. McGrawth, in *Michel Foucault: Ethics, Subjectivity and Truth*, ed. Paul Rabinow (New York: The New Press, 1997), 293.

10. See Ladelle McWhorter, *Bodies and Pleasures: Foucault and the Politics of Sexual Normalization* (Bloomington: Indiana University Press, 1999), 196; and Amy Allen, "Foucault, Feminism and the Self: The Politics of Personal Transformation," *Feminism and the Final Foucault*, eds. Dianna Taylor and Karen Vintges (Chicago: University of Illinois Press, 2004), 235–57.

MODULE 10
THE EVOLVING DEBATE

KEY POINTS

- Foucault's *Sexuality Vol. 1* has changed the way scholars think about sexuality, and influenced the development of new academic fields, including queer* theory and gender* and sexuality* studies.

- Foucault's ideas on power are, however, at odds with certain schools of thought—most notably, orthodox Marxism,* psychoanalysis,* and some branches of feminist* criticism, each of which is based on an idea of centralized power.

- Most recently, Foucault's concepts of biopower* and governmentality* have inspired the field of governmentality studies,* which uses his ideas to examine how liberal* societies are governed.

Uses and Problems

The History of Sexuality Vol. 1: The Will to Knowledge is one of Michel Foucault's most quoted and influential texts, and has had a considerable impact on the work of important thinkers and even whole intellectual schools. The scholars who are deeply engaged with the text are numerous and their activity ranges over diverse fields, from cultural studies* (a discipline proposing an anthropological* reading of social relations) and philosophy, to literature and anthropology.

However, the ideas Foucault advances in *Sexuality Vol. 1* are also at odds with certain schools of thought that take issue with Foucault's theory of power being dispersed (spread out). This argument conflicts with disciplines such as feminism, orthodox Marxism, and psychoanalysis, each of which is informed by a more centralized conception of power. Feminists see power in relation to male domination and a society's patriarchal* (male-ruled) views. For orthodox Marxists, power is concentrated in the hands of those with money and social status. For psychoanalysts, power shows itself in concepts such as the Law of the Father* (a term used by the French psychoanalyst Jacques Lacan* to describe the law prohibiting taboo actions such as incest). Each of these approaches is at odds with Foucault's views.

Feminist critics in particular, whose focus is closest to the subject matter of *Sexuality Vol. 1*, underline how Foucault's ideas are not suited for expressing resistance against patriarchy and male domination. Further, they point to the way Foucault is unclear in positions toward themes such as rape and sexual violence.

> *"Until Freud at least, the discourse on sex—the discourse of scholars and theoreticians—never ceased to hide the thing it was speaking about. We could take all these things that were said, the painstaking precautions and analyses, as so many procedures meant to evade the unbearable, too hazardous, truth of sex."*
>
> —— Michel Foucault, *The History of Sexuality Vol. 1: The Will to Knowledge*

Schools of Thought

Sexuality Vol. 1 does not belong to any one discipline. The text has fueled broad intellectual debate across the humanities* and social sciences* and radically changed the course of academic work on sexuality, power, and knowledge.

Scholars of queer theory and gender and sexuality studies have drawn from Foucault's ideas to question the standard sexual categories such as man/woman, and homosexual*/heterosexual.* Instead, they regard sexuality as "a historically singular experience"—something that changes and evolves depending on the historical period.[1] As the cultural historian Tamsin Spargo* argues in *Queer Studies and Foucault,* Foucault "can be seen as a catalyst [and] a point of departure" for queer theory, "an example and antecedent but also as a continuing irritant, a bit of grit that is still provoking the production of new ideas."[2] The American queer studies scholar David Halperin* likewise notes that, since the publication in English of *Sexuality Vol. 1* in 1978, progress in the field of sexuality studies "has been rapid and scholarly activity has been intense."[3]

Foucault's focus on the body is particularly useful here, as his move away from understanding individuals as stable beings with a given identity was a useful springboard for further study. It helped scholars who were trying to formulate a theory of sexual or gender oppression without accepting the idea that gender or sexual differences are fixed, natural identities.

Foucault's approach was of notable assistance to thinkers such as the US gender scholar Judith Butler* and Eve Sedgwick,* the authors of *Gender Trouble* (1990) and *Epistemology* of the Closet* (1990) respectively—among the first texts to introduce Foucault's

Sexuality Vol. 1 to university humanities departments, especially in the United States. Following Foucault's approach, both works attempt to challenge standard understandings of sexual categories (in Butler's case, male/ female; in Sedgwick's case, gay/straight). It is partly thanks to these books that Foucault is regarded as an intellectual father of queer theory and of gender and sexuality studies.

David Halperin has also helped popularize Foucault's ideas in academia. Among other titles, he wrote *One Hundred Years of Homosexuality and Other Essays on Greek Love* (1990), in which he employs a framework inspired by Foucault to examine the practices and values around sex between men in ancient Greece in contrast to those of bourgeois* (that is, modern Western) societies. With this book, and his biography *Saint Foucault: Toward a Gay Hagiography* (1995), Halperin has contributed to the spread of Foucault's ideas in the humanities.

In Current Scholarship

The ideas Foucault advanced in *Sexuality Vol. 1* have not only influenced academic debates about sexuality. Since the early 1990s, Foucault's ideas have been applied across the humanities and social sciences—and, most recently, in debates about governance.

Particularly noteworthy is Foucault's influence on the field known as governmentality studies—a term derived from Foucault's concept of governmentality that he developed in the last years of his life to describe the way power (which "governs") shapes subjects, or individuals, including their thoughts and beliefs ("mentality"). Although Foucault coined this term some years after the book's publication, *Sexuality Vol. 1* first advanced the ideas of dispersed power on which it is based. Foucault termed this power "biopower"*—that is to say, a power coming from "innumerable points, in the interplay of non-egalitarian [that is, unequal] and mobile [that is, changeable] relations" that seeks to regulate life.[4]

Governmentality studies, which is based on the work of a number of theorists, including the leading British sociologist Nikolas Rose,* borrows directly from Foucault's ideas. The field focuses on the ways that governance is exercised in liberal* societies ("liberal" is here used in the economic sense, describing the social consequence of the system of capitalism*). According to this school, power in liberal societies is not merely repressive and prohibiting but is distributed across institutions and mechanisms and uses techniques of governance that attempt to shape the conduct of the population. This idea draws directly from Foucault's understanding of how knowledge is produced, and from his claim that turning sex into an object of scientific analysis and using the findings from that research to categorize pathologies (illnesses) and perversions, finally led to new ways for the state to control its citizens.

Academic writing on governmentality in these fields has, in turn, led to renewed interest, since the early 2000s, on the relationship between power and the economy—and particularly on the economic doctrine of neoliberalism,*[5] according to which, government interference in the workings of the market and the national economy is to be discouraged, whatever the social consequences.

1. See Michel Foucault, *The History of Sexuality Vol 2: The Use of Pleasure*, trans. Robert Hurley (New York: Random House, 2012), 4.

2. Tamsin Spargo, *Foucault and Queer Theory.* (Cambridge: Icon books, 1999), 17; David Halperin, (New York: Oxford University Press, 1995), 10.

3. David Halperin, *One Hundred Years of Homosexuality: And Other Essays on Greek Love* (London: Routledge, 1990), 34.

4. Michel Foucault, *The History of Sexuality Vol. 1: The Will to knowledge*, trans. Robert Hurley (London: Penguin Books, 1998), 94.

5. See Wendy Larner, "Neo-liberalism: Policy, Ideology, Governmentality," *Studies in Political Economy* 63 (2000): 5–25; Nancy Fraser, "From Discipline to Flexibilization? Rereading Foucault in the Shadow of Globalization," *Constellations* 10, no. 2 (2003): 160–71.

MODULE 11
IMPACT AND INFLUENCE TODAY

KEY POINTS

* Foucault's *Sexuality Vol. 1* is a highly respected and widely cited text that has directly shaped academic debates around sexuality, and indirectly influenced the public understanding of gender* and sexual orientation.*

* Foucault's work is often cited as a prime example of poststructuralist* thought for its skepticism toward universal truths; this, however, puts it at odds with liberalism.*

* The controversy surrounding some of Foucault's ideas regarding sexuality, the binary models of man/woman or straight/gay, and the constructed nature of all knowledge are also what make his work a continuing source of interest.

Position

Michel Foucault's *The History of Sexuality Vol. 1: The Will to Knowledge* is considered a groundbreaking text across the humanities* and social sciences.* The work has been widely cited, and both its main and secondary ideas have been widely used across disciplines in the French-and English-speaking academic world. For instance, academic journals such as the *Journal of the History of Sexuality* and *Sexualities*, founded in 1990 and 1998 respectively, are heavily indebted to Foucault's method, scope, and approach. In addition, Foucault's ideas have shaped discussions about sexualities within gay, lesbian, and feminist communities, as well as in activist language and practice. The queer* theorist David Halperin* further notes that the politics of HIV* activists in the

1980s were strongly informed by *Sexuality Vol. 1.*[1]

While Foucault's line of reasoning in *Sexuality Vol. 1* is not widely known among the general public, for those familiar with his thought, his influence is clear in today's public debates about sexual minorities. In particular, Foucault's argument that sexuality is a product of social and historical circumstances, and not merely biologically determined, has greatly—if indirectly—influenced popular debates about gender identity* and sexual orientation. Moreover, the idea, largely associated with Foucault, that sexuality is used by institutions to control and make productive the lives of the population (for example, by championing reproduction and the nuclear family), has been highly influential within contemporary artistic production, such as in the work of the NewYork-based artist David Wojnarowicz.*[2]

Wojnarowicz was a prominent AIDS activist in the 1980s and 1990s. In his memoirs of this period chronicling his activism, Wojnarowicz wrote at length about his disgust with the marginalization and stigmatization of AIDS victims, particularly gay men, who were branded as a "risk" group. He built on Foucault's ideas about the way sexuality is used to diagnose people as "immoral" or "diseased," documenting the way AIDS was employed by politicians to justify demonizing homosexuals.*

Foucault's work has also been itself the subject of artistic production, for example the 1993 BBC documentary *Michel Foucault: Beyond Good and Evil* that offers a portrait of Foucault's life and work,[3] or the acclaimed art installation 24h Foucault by the Swiss artist Thomas Hirschhorn.*[4]

The book's relevance extends beyond its immediate subject matter. This is the case in particular for the arguments Foucault put forward in the last two parts of *Sexuality Vol. 1*: part 4 "The Deployment of Sexuality" and part 5 "Right of Death and Power over Life," where he analyzed the idea of power in modern societies. This has influenced debates in the medical sciences, such as clinical psychiatry,* regarding the way health care is linked to society's systems of social control.[5]

> "We must ... abandon the hypothesis that modern industrial societies ushered in an age of increased sexual repression. We have not only witnessed a visible explosion of unorthodox sexualities; but—and this is the important point—a deployment quite different from the law, even if it is locally dependent on procedures of prohibition, has ensured ... the proliferation of specific pleasures and the multiplication of disparate sexualities. It has been said that ... the agencies of power [have] taken such care to feign ignorance of the thing they prohibited ... But ... the opposite ... has become apparent."
>
> —— Michel Foucault, *The History of Sexuality Vol. 1: The Will to Knowledge*

Interaction

Among the schools of thought most skeptical about Foucault's work is that of liberalism; social liberals are concerned with the progression of civil rights, democracy, and social equality. Liberal approaches value factors such as rationality, choice, autonomy (the

ability to act without coercion), and equal rights. Liberal feminists,*
for instance, insist that women and men should be given the
same opportunities in society, believing that promoting women's
social inclusion (including in the work place) will advance gender
equality. This view assumes certain universal truths, for example
that men and women are equal, and that all human beings deserve
basic rights. It is incompatible with poststructuralism (including
Foucault's approach—*Sexuality Vol. 1* is often taken to be a good
example of poststructuralist thought), which mistrusts universal,
humanist values and contends that all so-called "truths" are in fact
dependent on other factors.

For the same reason, liberal feminists have often criticized
Foucault and his followers for supposedly not having anything in
their theoretical approach that would support women's struggles
against gender inequality and patriarchy.* Foucault claims that
the way we understand gender categories is the product of a social
construct and not derived from the actual biological differences
between the two genders. This challenges the liberal belief in the
existence of two naturally separate and opposed sexes, male and
female.

Liberal feminists also criticize Foucault's anti-essentialist*
ideas (that is, his belief that there are no deep, real differences, such
as male/female or straight/gay). For example, the American law
and philosophy professor Martha Nussbaum,* in her 1999 article
"The Professor of Parody: The Hip Defeatism of Judith Butler,*"
forcefully attacked the tendency in feminist thought to follow
Foucault. Nussbaum critiques the feminist theorist Judith Butler

who, she argues, "seems to many young scholars to define what feminism is now."[6] She also attacks Foucault for not being able to come up with a concept of resistance against oppression. Nussbaum argues that Foucault's approaches to sexuality lack "a normative theory of social justice and human dignity"[7] leading to "quietism [calm acceptance] and retreat."[8]

The Continuing Debate

Foucault's contribution stands as a lasting challenge to all theoretical traditions that treat sexual behavior as something biologically determined. More particularly, *Sexuality Vol. 1* confronts positivist* disciplines such as biology or, for that matter, biological anthropology* ("positivist" here refers to the position that knowledge derives from observation; "biological anthropology" is a field that concerns the study of human behavior in the light of our deep history and nature as an organism). Both disciplines see sexual orientation, preferences, and tastes as biological and evolutionary factors. Those inspired by Foucault's work, by contrast, question the existence of a natural or true human nature. Like Foucault, they prefer to speak about how particular types of knowledge about sex occur, and how these in turn inform our desires and ways of practicing and thinking about sex.

In relation to the above, we can claim that Foucault radically challenges liberal schools of thought and, in this case, liberal approaches to sexuality. Without denying the need for political action and resistance to oppression, Foucault's work has helped confront the use of essentialism* (the view that there is such a thing as an essential human nature) to demand human rights.[9] These challenges are very much in the spirit of Foucault, who preferred to contest ideas usually taken for granted by putting them into a historical context and raising questions about them.

---

1. See Ann Laura Stoler, *Race and the Education of Desire: Foucault's History of Sexuality and the Colonial Order of Things* (Durham, North Carolina: Duke University Press, 1995), 1–2.

2. See Thomas Roach, "Sense and Sexuality: Foucault, Wojnarowicz, and Biopower," *Nebula: A Journal of Multidisciplinary Scholarship* 6, no. 3 (2009): 155–73.

3. "Michel Foucault: Beyond Good and Evil," BFI, 1993, accessed March 6, 2016, http: //www.bfi.org. uk/films-tv-people/4ce2b7c9bb0c5.

4. Thomas Hirschhorn, "24h Foucault", October 1, 2004, accessed March 6, 2016, http: //1995–2015. undo.net/it/mostra/21388.

5. See Robin Bunton and Alan Petersen, eds., *Foucault, Health and Medicine* (London: Routledge, 2002); Jennifer Radden, *The Philosophy of Psychiatry: A Companion* (Oxford: Oxford University Press, 2004), 248–9; Ann Branaman, "Contemporary Social Theory and the Sociological Study of Mental Health," in *Mental Health, Social Mirror*, eds. William R. Avison et al. (New York: Springer, 2007), 95–126; Ann Rogers and David Pilgrim, *A Sociology of Mental Health and Illness* (Maidenhead: Open University Press, 2014), 37–52.

6. Martha Nussbaum, "The Professor of Parody," *The New Republic* 22, no. 2 (1999): 38.

7. Nussbaum, "The Professor of Parody," 40.

8. Nussbaum, "The Professor of Parody," 38.

9. See Irene Diamond and Lee Quinby, eds., *Feminism & Foucault: Reflections on Resistance* (Boston: Northeastern University Press, 1988), 7.

MODULE 12
WHERE NEXT?

KEY POINTS

- Foucault's *Sexuality Vol. 1* continues to influence contemporary scholarship, most recently in debates about governance and globalization (the tightening of economic, cultural, and governmental connections across continental boundaries).

- Foucault's ideas are likely to continue being used in the discussion of gay marriage and gay rights, as well as in academic studies of social power structures across the ages.

- *Sexuality Vol. 1* marked an important moment in the history of the humanities* and social sciences,* highlighting the extent to which knowledge itself is produced, and academic analyses shaped by the cultural and historical context in which they are written.

Potential

Michel Foucault's *The History of Sexuality Vol. 1: The Will to Knowledge* has proved relevant to new social and historical situations, and to issues he could not have foreseen. For instance, the social theorists Antonio Negri* and Michael Hardt's* Empire (2000) uses Foucault's concepts of biopolitics* and biopower* to trace the shift from the traditional rule of kings and queens and the traditional nation-state to a world order made up of multinational corporations and transnational government organizations (such as the United Nations).[*1]

In *Sexuality Vol. 1*, Foucault argued that forces that he labeled "biopolitical" aim to regulate social life and that the language used around sexuality* was one of the most important of these forces. Negri and Hardt modify Foucault's ideas: they argue that sexuality is less important a subject for regulating social life today, and insist instead that biopolitical control is linked to the economic processes of globalization. This change to Foucault's arguments partly reflects the fact that sexual minorities in the West are treated better than they were in the mid-1970s when *Sexuality Vol. 1* was written. Perhaps more importantly, it shows how Foucault's ideas are rich and flexible enough to examine issues (such as globalization) that were only just emerging when he was alive.

> "When I read—and I know that it has been attributed to me— the thesis that 'knowledge is power' or 'power is knowledge,' I begin to laugh, since studying their relation is precisely my problem. If they were identical, I would not have to study them and I would be spared a lot of fatigue as a result. The very fact that I pose the question of their relation proves clearly that I do not identify them as the same."
>
> —— Michel Foucault, as cited in Gérard Raulet, "Structuralism and Poststructuralism: An Interview with Michel Foucault"

Future Directions

Foucault's text remains a vital reference in academic and popular debates on topics such as gender,* sexuality,* feminism* and gay activism. Especially in fields such as queer* theory and gender* and sexuality studies, the book enjoys high visibility and figures as a constant reference on college syllabuses and in new publications.

As the cultural theorist Tamsin Spargo* notes in her book *Foucault and Queer Theory* (1999), both Foucault himself and his writing on sexuality have served as "a powerful model for many gay, lesbian and other intellectuals."[2] As such, we can safely conclude that *Sexuality Vol. 1* will continue to exert an influence as a key text for debates on the way sexual orientations and gender identities are defined and put into categories—and whether these categories are even necessary.

Efforts in the last decade to use Foucault's ideas in discussions over the legalization of gay marriage in the United States, for instance, suggest the lasting relevance of his ideas now and in future discussions of gay, lesbian, and transsexual* rights (the rights of those who feels that the gender they were assigned at birth is incorrect). In his "The Foucauldian-Marxist Conflict: Exploitation and Power in Gay Marriage" (2006), commentator Nick Stone notes that Foucault "would have been far more concerned [by] the pervasiveness of the current debate over gay marriage than with the issue itself, as the very nature of this debate serves as partial confirmation of his theories [regarding] repression and sexuality."[3] He suggests that *Sexuality Vol. 1* offers a way into thinking about the evolution of the debate over gay marriage, including how its supporters and opponents have framed their arguments, as well as how big the issue has become in public debate, noting, "That the national attention would be captured by the issue of homosexuality* in the midst of two foreign wars and serious economic troubles is a major validation of Foucault's thesis: that Western society cannot avoid being drawn to discuss its sexuality."[4]

The use of Foucault's concept of biopolitics also continues. Perhaps the most notable of these is the Italian philosopher Giorgio Agamben's* "Homo Sacer Project," which he began writing in the mid-1990s. So far, Agamben has completed seven books in the series, including *Homo Sacer* (1995), *State of Exception* (2003), and, most recently, *The Highest Poverty: Monastic Rules and Form-of-Life* (2013). The last of these is a genealogical* study, in the spirit of Foucault, of the creation of written rules in the fourth century, and their eventual development into law. As with the discussion of Foucault's ideas in relation to gay marriage, Agamben's work shows how Foucault's ideas are readily adaptable to new issues.

Summary

Sexuality Vol. 1 is a key text in the humanities and social sciences. Foucault overturned the long-held view of eighteenth- and nineteenth-century society as sexually repressive. But he also showed how this view was merely a variation of a dominant position, promoted by scientific institutions such as psychiatry* and biology,* that had been pushing people to put sex into words since the eighteenth century. That is, he showed how the discussion around sexual liberation was a product of the very same institutions that first sought to study sexual behavior and regulate it.

Foucault's text laid the foundations for many fields of inquiry, including gender and sexuality studies, queer theory, and governmentality studies.* It deserves special attention for the central position it now occupies in various debates concerning politics, education, sexuality, and activism. It can also be seen as belonging to and influencing different fields of study, from literature and philosophy to sociology* and anthropology.*

As its title reminds us, however, *Sexuality Vol. 1* must be considered in the light of the discipline of history. Even though, as the history professor Allan Megill argues, "a gulf separates him from [the academic discipline of] history,"[5] Foucault's work stirred important and sharp debates among historians.[6] His work challenged the idea that the past can be understood in its entirety, let alone recounted in a unified way. Instead, he showed how our deeper beliefs inform our understanding of the past, leading us to interpret it in one way and not another. By revealing how sexuality has been studied by Western scientists, and by showing the categories, norms, and rules that have been established on the basis of those studies, Foucault also demonstrated the extent to which knowledge informs culture, shapes identities, and upholds power structures. These ideas, which were truly novel for their time, continue to influence academics' debates about power, governance, and knowledge.

---

1. Michael Hardt and Antonio Negri, *Empire*. Cambridge: Harvard University Press, 2000.

2. Tamsin Spargo, *Foucault and Queer Theory* (Cambridge: Icon books, 1999), 8.

3. Nick Stone, "The Foucauldian-Marxist Conflict: Exploitation and Power in Gay Marriage," *Discoveries* 7 (2006): 66, accessed November 15, 2015, http: //www.arts.cornell.edu/knight_institute/ publicationsprizes/discoveries/ discoveriesspring2006/06stone.pdf.

4. Stone, "The Foucauldian-Marxist Conflict," 70.

5. Allan Megill, "The Reception of Foucault by Historians," *Journal of the History of Ideas* 48 (1987): 117.

6. Mark Poster, *Foucault, Marxism, and History: Mode of Production Versus Mode of Information* (Cambridge: Polity Press, 1984).

GLOSSARY OF TERMS

1. **AIDS (Acquired Immune Deficiency Syndrome):** an illness caused by HIV (human immunodeficiency virus) first observed in Congo in 1959 and in the United States in 1981. Foucault died of AIDS. He and his writings on sexuality influenced activists in the 1980s who sought to spread awareness of the disease and overturn the view that only gay men were at risk of catching it.

2. **Anarchist political theory:** a branch of political theory that advocates self-governance through nonhierarchical institutions sometimes referred to as stateless societies.

3. **Androcentric:** focusing on the experience of men.

4. **Annales School:** a method and style of history writing developed in France in the twentieth century mainly around the journal *Annales: Economies, Sociétés, Civilisations. Annales* used social-scientific methods to focus on social rather than diplomatic or political issues.

5. **Anthropology:** the study of humans and human behavior and their cultures. The field draws on a number of other fields in the physical, biological, and social sciences and humanities.

6. **Anti-essentialism:** the intellectual tradition that rejects the existence of a natural essence, or identity, in people or things (Foucault's claim, for example, that sexual identity is not instinctive, but socially constructed).

7. *The Archaeology of Knowledge* **(1969):** a book by Michel Foucault. Archaeology is the analysis of artifacts and ruins to understand past human activity and the societies from which they came. Foucault used the term in this book, and in the first half of his career, to refer to his approach to historical research: examining traces of past discourses and systems provides a way to understand the processes that have brought us to where we are today.

8. **Ars erotica (art of pleasure):** a Latin term Foucault uses to refer to the view of sex as an art form, which he distinguishes from the Western's scientific approach to sex as an object of knowledge: *scientia sexualis.*

9. **Biological anthropology:** a branch of anthropology that examines human evolution and ecology in relation to evolutionary history and biology, and

that assumes human behavior is partly rooted in certain innate, hereditary, characteristics. These ideas are at odds with Foucault's theories, which assume that all human behavior is socially constructed.

10. **Biology:** a natural science that studies living things, including the function, structure, growth, evolution, taxonomy, and distribution of living organisms.

11. **Biopolitics:** Foucault's term for political strategies that aim to regulate and control the life of populations. He sees biopolitics as a typical type of governance in modern societies.

12. **Biopower:** a term Foucault coined, in *The History of Sexuality,* to describe "an explosion of numerous and diverse techniques for achieving the subjugation of bodies and the control of populations." The term describes how the state regulates its subjects by regulating, among other things, health, sexuality, heredity, and so on.

13. ***The Birth of the Clinic* (1963):** one of Foucault's early writings. The book examines the history of modern medicine through the creation of the clinic in order to consider how pathologies (diseases) are categorized and how culture and customs influence our understanding of health. As with all of Foucault's work, the book is interested in how knowledge and truth are constructed.

14. **Bourgeoisie:** a term used in classical Marxist theory to refer to people in a capitalist economy who own the means of production—landowners, factory owners, and other employers who in turn wield power over workers of the lower classes (known as proletariats). The bourgeoisie are generally assumed to abuse their power and exploit the proletariat (the working people).

15. **Capitalism:** an economic system in which the means of production, trade, and industry are privately owned and conducted for private profit.

16. **Colonialism:** refers to the rule of one country by another, involving unequal power relations between the ruler (colonial power) and ruled (colony), and the exploitation of the colonies' resources to strengthen the economy of the colonizers' home country.

17. **Cultural studies:** an intellectual school that first emerged in Britain during

the 1960s and then spread internationally. Cultural studies propose an anthropological reading of social relations, examining culture as a form of lived experience.

18. **Demography:** the study, usually using statistics, of the life-conditions of communities of people, be they the population of a city, a country, a neighborhood, or a specific institution such as a prison or university.

19. ***Discipline and Punish* (1975):** a text in which Foucault explores the transformations of the penal system in Western modernity.

20. **Epistemology:** term used to refer to the study of knowledge; the methods used to attain knowledge; and the basis of knowledge.

21. **Essentialism:** the view that all entities—animal, human being, group of people, physical object, idea—have certain qualities that are necessary to their identity and function. Foucault's work is anti-essentialist in that it questions whether there is such a thing as "human nature," or whether all humans share a specific human essence.

22. **Eurocentrism:** the tendency to believe that European culture is superior or more important than others. In scholarship, a Eurocentric work would be one that assumes a European perspective without acknowledging others.

23. **Feminism:** a series of ideologies and movements concerned with equal social, political, cultural, and economic rights for women, including equal rights in the home, workplace, education, and government.

24. **Feminist, queer, gay, and lesbian studies:** all these fields explore the ways that gender, sex, and sexual orientation are shaped by society and social norms.

25. **Freudo-Marxism:** theoretical approaches that combine Marxist critiques of capitalism with Freudian psychoanalysis. Some of the most notable Freudo-Marxist thinkers are Herbert Marcuse and Wilhelm Reich.

26. **Gender identity:** a person's individual experience of their gender—that is, of being a man or a woman, and of belonging to the category of male or female. A person might also have an ambiguous gender identity, or be uncertain of their gender identity.

27. **Gender studies:** the inquiry into the ways that gender—the sum of attributes considered to represent identities such as "male" or "female"—is constituted by society.

28. **Genealogy:** Foucault uses the German philosopher Nietzsche's idea of "genealogy" to describe his historical method. Genealogy examines concepts and practices within social settings without searching for their origin or inner truth. Instead, it examines these practices in relation to each other, and understands them to be dependent on each other—that is, influencing and shaping the outcomes of others.

29. **Governmentality:** practices of governing that aim to shape citizens' conduct instead of openly suppressing them. The term, coined by Foucault, helps us to understand how power works in modern societies.

30. **Governmentality studies:** a field that applies Foucault's concept of governmentality to understand how governance works in modern liberal societies, including in health care, in relation to migration and asylum issues, and in the arena of crime control.

31. **Great Refusal:** one of Herbert Marcuse's key concepts, it refers to opposition to and protest against unnecessary repression, and the struggle for the ultimate form of freedom—"to live without anxiety."

32. **Hermaphrodism:** a term used to refer to the presence of both, or a combination of, male and female organs in the same individual.

33. **Heteronormativity/heterosexuality:** the view that all human beings fit into distinct gender categories (man and woman) with corresponding natural roles, and that heterosexuality is the only normal, or natural, sexual orientation.

34. **Heterosexuality:** the sexual and/or romantic attraction to those of the opposite sex.

35. **HIV:** human immunodeficiency virus, the viral agent that causes the disease AIDS.

36. ***The History of Sexuality Vol. 2*** **(1984):** the second volume of Foucault's study of sexuality, which examines the topic in ancient Greece, focusing

specifically on the concept of pleasure, its social role, and its regulation.

37. ***The History of Sexuality Vol. 3* (1984):** the third and last volume of Foucault's study of sexuality, which examines the topic in ancient Rome, focusing specifically on the concept of self-care.

38. **Homosexuality:** the sexual and/or romantic attraction to those of one's same sex.

39. **Humanities:** a broad term used to define academic disciplines relating to the study of human culture, including history, literature and literary criticism, anthropology, classics, geography, languages, law, music, theater, dance, philosophy, religion, and visual culture (film, drawing, sculpture, painting, gaming).

40. **Hysteria:** a term used in the nineteenth century to describe the physical display of psychological stress, most often in women. Foucault examines the origins of the term and its role in regulating, among other things, women's sexual desire.

41. **Law of the Father:** a phrase coined by the French psychoanalyst and philosopher Jacques Lacan to describe the law prohibiting incest, which ushers the child into the system of rules and prohibitions that regulate social bonds.

42. **Leftist:** a term used to refer to individuals or communities that hold left-wing political views, or to describe those views. Left-wing or leftist views tend to advocate change and reform in the interest of promoting equality.

43. **Liberal feminism:** an individualistic branch of feminism that assumes women can attain equality through personal actions and choices.

44. **Liberalism:** a term with different connotations in fields such as economics, society, and international relations. In a social sense, "liberalism" refers to the advocacy of civil liberties and individual rights, and political reform aimed at improving democracy and individual freedom; in an economic sense, it refers to the capitalist principle of market freedom.

45. **Linguist:** a student of linguistics (the study of the nature, functioning, and structure of languages).

46. ***Madness and Civilization* (1964):** an early work by Michel Foucault that

examines the origins of the modern notion of insanity, relating it to the development of scientific thought following the Enlightenment. Foucault's ultimate point is to show the sociocultural roots of our understanding of mental illness.

47. **Marxism:** the intellectual and political movements built around the writings of the nineteenth-century philosopher and economist Karl Marx.

48. **May 1968:** a period of massive civil unrest in France that involved protests, strikes, occupations of schools and factories, and riots inspired by Marxist ideas of a more just society.

49. **Medical gaze:** a term Foucault uses to denote the dehumanizing, clinical approach that medical doctors have when treating patients, which consists of treating the body and mind as separate entities.

50. **Middle Ages:** a term used to refer to the period in European history between the fall of the Roman Empire (circa 500 c.e.) and the beginning of the Renaissance (fourteenth century).

51. **Modernity:** the intellectual response to the sociocultural changes that occurred from the late seventeenth century onwards, including industrialization, the growth of cities, the rise of the nation state, and political democracy. The concept came to be associated with the replacement of traditional values and beliefs by new ideals based on science, reason, and liberalism.

52. **Neoliberalism:** a political economic theory and practice that favors entrepreneurial freedoms, privatization, and market deregulation, while giving less attention to social welfare.

53. **Neurology:** the study of the brain and nervous system.

54. ***On the Genealogy of Morals: A Polemic* (1887):** a book by Friedrich Nietzsche, in which he traces the origins of moral concepts. Much of Foucault's work is based on, or elaborates, the ideas advanced in Nietzsche's text.

55. ***The Order of Things: An Archaeology of the Human Sciences* (1966):** a book by Michel Foucault that (borrowing the language of archaeology) seeks to excavate the origins of the human sciences and, in particular, sociology and psychology. As with Foucault's other works, it is above all concerned with how

knowledge is constructed and our assumptions about truth; however, it differs from his late work in its specifically structuralist approach.

56. **Orthodox Marxism:** refers to narrow interpretations of Marx, mostly related to the prominent role that economics plays in social relations.

57. **Pathology:** a broad term for any psychological or physical medical disorder or suffering. Pathological behavior refers to behavior that reflects an underlying mental disorder. Much of Foucault's work was concerned with how pathologies are defined and what those definitions say about the surrounding culture.

58. **Patriarchy:** social organizations (governments, families, and other communities) ruled by males, in which descent is reckoned through the male line, and children are given the father's last name.

59. **Pedagogy:** the practice of teaching and the theories or principles on which education is based.

60. **Phenomenology:** a branch of philosophy that developed in the eighteenth century. It studies the structures that inform our experience and our consciousness of the world around us, and the role that perception plays in the way we relate to the world.

61. **Polymorphous:** something that assumes, has, or occurs in different or varying forms, characters, or styles. Foucault claims that power is polymorphous in that it assumes different forms.

62. **Positivism:** a philosophical school that holds that what one observes can be a legitimate source of human knowledge. By putting emphasis on the empirical (that which is based on experiment or observation), and on what is experienced as holding a particular "truth," positivist scholarship generally avoids looking at how subjectivities are mediated and defined by culture, ideology, and language.

63. **Postcolonial studies:** an academic discipline that studies the effects of colonialism and imperialism on once-colonized cultures and populations, before or after political "independence." It draws from a range of disciplines and schools of thought, especially from poststructuralism, critical theory, Marxist theory, and anthropology.

64. **Post-Marxism:** a social theory and philosophy grounded in Marxism that extends, reverses, or modifies it. Contemporary post-Marxists who often employ Foucault's arguments include Ernesto Laclau, Chantal Mouffe, and Antonio Negri.

65. **Poststructuralism:** a label invented to refer to the work of a mainly French group of theorists and philosophers of the 1960s and 1970s who regarded social structures and categories as basically unstable. Although Foucault was often thought of as a poststructuralist, he rejected the label.

66. **Prison Information Group:** a group founded in 1971 in France that attempted to bring radio and newspapers into prisons to expose the conditions. It published four journals attempting to "turn the prison inside out," publishing information that attempted to make prison officials rather than prisoners the targets of unwanted attention.

67. **Psychiatry:** the branch of medicine that deals in the study, treatment, and prevention of mental disorders.

68. **Psychoanalysis:** a theory and method conceived by Sigmund Freud in the late nineteenth century that seeks to understand the human psyche and treat mental disorders.

69. **Psychology:** an academic and applied discipline dealing with the study and treatment of mental behavior and mental functions.

70. **Queer theory:** an academic field that emerged in North American humanities departments in the 1990s and then spread mainly throughout the English-speaking academic world. Queer theory wishes to disturb traditional sexual and other categories.

71. **Repressive hypothesis:** the title of one of the chapters in Michel Foucault's *The History of Sexuality Vol. 1,* and a term he uses throughout the book to describe a particular set of beliefs regarding sexuality's role throughout history, which were advanced by Freudo-Marxist academics in the 1960s and 1970s, as well as by post-May 1968 advocates of sexual liberation.

72. **Roman Catholic confession:** a religious rite in which an individual tells a priest

his or her sins—things they have done that go against Christian teachings—and ask for God's forgiveness.

73. **Roman Catholicism:** a broad term used to define traditions specific to the Roman Catholic Church, including (but not limited to) their doctrine, ethics, and theology.

74. **Sexuality studies:** an academic field that explores the ways that sexual identities are constituted in society at large, in spheres such as cinema, art, popular culture, literature, and politics.

75. **Sexual orientation:** a term used to refer to a person's sexual identity in relation to the gender to which they are attracted. Heterosexual, homosexual, and bisexual are all sexual orientations.

76. **Social sciences:** a broad term that groups academic disciplines examining society and human relationships within society, including economics, history, law, psychology, sociology, political science, education, geography, and anthropology.

77. **Sociology:** the academic study of social behavior. The discipline examines the origins and development of social relations, their different modes of organization, and different social institutions.

78. **Structuralism:** a theoretical approach arguing that elements of culture become intelligible if studied in relation to the larger structures and systems to which they belong. It originated in the linguistics of Ferdinand de Saussure and was later developed by, among others, the anthropologist Claude Lévi-Strauss.

79. **Subjectivity:** a concept used to explain differences between individuals (including tastes, opinions, values, and beliefs), and to account for the distance between a person's views and those of their surrounding community. In philosophy, the concept is crucial to the discussion of why people are so different in the way they interpret and relate to the world around them.

80. **Theology:** the systematic study of religious ideas, usually conducted through readings of scripture.

81. **Transsexual:** a person who feels that the gender they were assigned at birth

(on the basis of their genitals) is incorrect. A transsexual may choose to undergo gender-reassignment surgery and hormone therapy to become the gender they feel they are.

82. **United Nations:** an international body instituted following World War II designed to foster communication, cooperation, and security between nations; its headquarters is in New York.

83. **Victorian morality:** the moral values that prevailed at the time of Queen Victoria's reign in Great Britain from 1837 to 1901. These moral values involved strict rules of social conduct, like sexual constraints and a prohibition against scandalous language.

84. **Vietnam War (1955–1975):** a conflict fought in Vietnam that also involved Laos and Cambodia. It pitted the nationalist South Vietnam against the communist North Vietnam. Opposition to France's role in the war was among the causes of unrest in the events leading up to May 1968.

85. **Will to power:** an important concept developed by Friedrich Nietzsche that he used to describe what he thought was the motivating force in humans: ambition and the desire to achieve the highest possible position available to them.

86. **World War I (1914–1918):** A global war between two alliances: the Central Powers (Germany and Austria-Hungary) and the Allies (the Russian Empire, the British Empire, and France).

1. **Giorgio Agamben (b. 1942)** is an important contemporary Italian philosopher and political theorist working in the fields of linguistics, law, and politics. Some of his most well-known works are *Homo Sacer* (1998) and *State of Exception* (2005).

2. **Louis Althusser (1918–90)** was a French Marxist philosopher who is often associated today with the school of structuralism. However, Althusser was critical of certain aspects of structuralist thought, and spent his life supporting the central tenets of Marxism. Foucault was greatly influenced by Althusser's work.

3. **Judith Butler (b. 1956)** is an influential American theorist and academic whose work has significantly shaped fields such as feminist and queer theory. Her most notable books include *Gender Trouble* (1990) and *Bodies That Matter* (1993).

4. **James Clifford (b. 1945)** is an American anthropologist.

5. **Jacques Derrida (1930–2004)** was a French philosopher best known for his work in the development of "deconstruction," a form of semiotic analysis, and for his involvement in the schools of structuralism and poststructuralism. Derrida and Foucault hugely disagreed in their critical approaches, and it has been said that Foucault wrote some of his books as a direct response to Derrida's criticisms.

6. **Epictetus (55–135 c.e.)** was a Greek-speaking philosopher who lived in Rome, and who championed philosophy as a way of life, not just a theoretical discipline. Foucault makes frequent reference to Epictetus's ideas about morality, death, independence, and selfhood in *The History of Sexuality Vol. 3*.

7. **Sigmund Freud (1856–1939)** was an Austrian neurologist who pioneered the view that human actions are driven in large part by unconscious desires and primordial urges. He is the founder of psychoanalysis.

8. **David M. Halperin (b. 1952)** is an American scholar specializing in the fields of queer theory, queer studies, critical theory, visual culture, and material culture. He is best known for his book *One Hundred Years of Homosexuality* (1990), in which he argues the historical significance of the use of the term "homosexual" by Richard von Krafft-Ebing in the study of sexual pathologies, *Psycopathia Sexualis,* which was translated into English in 1892. Halperin has also written

extensively on Foucault and his influence on queer studies.

9. **Michael Hardt (b. 1960)** is an American Marxist/post-Marxist literary theorist and political philosopher best known for coauthoring *Empire* (2000) with Antonio Negri, a book that applies Foucault's concepts of biopower and biopolitics to examine how power operates in the post-Cold War, globalized economy.

10. **Thomas Hirschhorn (b. 1957)** is a Swiss artist known for his politically charged art installations that often pay tribute to seminal left-wing thinkers. To date he has created works inspired by Antonio Gramsci, Gilles Deleuze, and Michel Foucault. His *24h Foucault,* an art installation featuring (among other things) a library, shop, bar, and auditorium, sought to create a space for viewers akin to the inside of Foucault's brain.

11. **Jean Hyppolite (1907–68)** was a French philosopher and follower of Georg Hegel and the German philosophical movement, and a prominent figure in French thinking in the mid-twentieth century. Foucault studied under him and was profoundly shaped by his ideas on the relationship between history and philosophy.

12. **Jacques Lacan (1901–81)** was a French psychoanalyst and psychiatrist best known for advocating a "return to Freud" through a close reading of his texts and a redress of the way in which Freud's theories had been misunderstood and perverted by his followers, especially in the United States. Lacanian psychoanalysis had a profound influence on French philosophy and feminist theory.

13. **Ernesto Laclau (1935–2014)** was an Argentine post-Marxist political theorist. He is best known for *Hegemony and Socialist Strategy* (1985), which he coauthored with Chantal Mouffe, and for his first book, *Politics and Ideology in Marxist Theory* (1977). Laclau was greatly influenced by Foucault's writings on power.

14. **Claude Lévi-Strauss (1908–2009)** was a French ethnologist and anthropologist, and is frequently cited as the "father of modern anthropology." His work is based on the application of the structural linguistic theories of Ferdinand de Saussure to anthropology.

15. **Herbert Marcuse (1898–1979)** was an influential American-based German philosopher and prominent member of the Frankfurt School working at the intersection of Marxism and psychoanalysis. His best known works include *Eros and Civilization* (1955) and *One-Dimensional Man* (1964).

16. **Biddy Martin (b. 1951)** is an American writer and intellectual known for her writings on feminism and queer theory—most notably, *Femininity Played Straight: The Significance of Being Lesbian* (1996). Martin has been critical of Foucault's work, arguing that his views on sexuality are androcentric, and do not lend themselves to feminist applications.

17. **Karl Marx (1818–83)** was a German political philosopher and economist whose analysis of class relations under capitalism and articulation of a more egalitarian system provided the basis for communism. Together with Friedrich Engels (1820–1895), Marx wrote *The Communist Manifesto* (1848). He articulated his full theory of production and class relations in *Das Kapital* (1867).

18. **Maurice Merleau-Ponty (1908–61)** was a French phenomenological philosopher and writer, and the only major philosopher of his time to incorporate descriptive psychology in his work. This influenced later phenomenologists, who went on to use cognitive science and psychology in their studies.

19. **Chantal Mouffe (b. 1943)** is a Belgian political theorist best known for developing, together with Ernesto Laclau, the school of discourse analysis— an approach to post-Marxist political inquiry that draws on poststructuralist ideas, including Foucault's. She and Laclau coauthored *Hegemony and Socialist Strategy* (1985), the text credited with laying the grounds of discourse analysis.

20. **Antonio Negri (b. 1933)** is an Italian Marxist/post-Marxist philosopher best known for coauthoring *Empire* (2000) with Michael Hardt. Negri uses Foucault's concepts of biopower and biopolitics in much of his writing.

21. **Friedrich Nietzsche (1844–1900)** was a prominent German philosopher who radically questioned concepts such as religion, morality, and truth.

22. **Martha Nussbaum (b. 1947)** is an American philosopher. She is professor of law and ethics at the University of Chicago.

23. **Monique Plaza** is a French feminist writer and thinker, and cofounder of the influential French journal *Questiones Feministes*, which first published in 1980. Plaza was an outspoken critic of Foucault.

24. **Plutarch (46–120 c.e.)** was a Greek essayist, historian, and biographer. Foucault wrote about Plutarch's work on love and sex in *The History of Sexuality Vol. 3.*

25. **Wilhelm Reich (1897–1957)** was a radical Austrian psychoanalyst who wrote extensively on the effects of sexual repression. His most notable works include *The Mass Psychology of Fascism* (1933) and *The Sexual Revolution* (1936).

26. **Nikolas Rose (b. 1947)** is an influential British social theorist and sociologist who has written on mental health policy and risk, the sociology and history of psychiatry, and the social implications of new psychopharmacological developments in the area of mental health. He is best known for his writings on Foucault and for reviving interest in Foucault's concept of governmentality in the Anglophone world.

27. **Ferdinand de Saussure (1857–1913)** was a Swiss linguist whose ideas on structure in language laid the foundation for the linguistic sciences in the twentieth century.

28. **Alan D. Schrift** is an American professor of nineteenth-and twentieth-century French and German philosophy at Grinnell College, Iowa. He has written extensively on Foucault.

29. **Eve Sedgwick (1950–2009)** was an influential American theorist and university professor in the fields of queer theory and gender studies. Her most celebrated work is *Epistemology of the Closet* (1990).

30. **Seneca (4 b.c.e.–65 c.e.)** was Roman philosopher, tutor to the emperor Nero, and proponent of the philosophical school of Stoicism; Foucault discussed him in *The History of Sexuality Vol. 3*. Foucault's work on Seneca's idea of the "care of the self" caused scholars to revise their assessment of the work.

31. **Tamsin Spargo** is a cultural historian specializing in queer theory, queer culture, gender, and countercultural literature.

32. **Gayatri Chakravorty Spivak (b. 1942)** is an Indian theorist and philosopher,

whose work has proved extremely influential within the discipline of postcolonial studies. One of her most widely read texts is the essay "Can the Subaltern Speak?" (1988).

33. **Ann Stoler (b. 1949)** is an American anthropologist best known for her writings on the sexual politics of empire (how sexuality and gender are treated under colonial rule), as well as issues of colonial governance. She was among the first academics to point out Foucault's failure to mention colonialism as a decisive factor in his account of sexuality in modern Western culture.

34. **Fathi Triki (b. 1947)** is a French philosopher and emeritus professor at the University of Tunisia. He studied under Foucault and was greatly influenced by his ideas.

35. **Carl Westphal (1833–90)** was a German psychiatrist best known for coining the term "agoraphobia"—the fear of large, open spaces—and credited, by Foucault, for creating the term "homosexual," which influenced the modern definition of homosexuality as something tied to one's identity. Westphal considered homosexuality to be a psychiatric disorder.

36. **David Wojnarowicz (1954–92)** was a gay artist, writer, filmmaker, photographer, and AIDS activist best known for his involvement in the New York City art scene of the 1970s and 1980s, and for his often controversial art installations that sought to challenge the stigmatization of homosexuality and AIDS. He is frequently discussed by queer theorists in relation to Foucault's work.

 **WORKS CITED**

1. Afary, Janet, and Kevin B. Anderson. "Foucault, Gender and Male Homosexualities in Mediterranean and Muslim Society." In *Foucault and the Iranian Revolution: Gender and the Seductions of Islamism,* 138–62. Chicago: Chicago University Press, 2005.

2. Agamben, Giorgio. *The Highest Poverty: Monastic Rules and Form-of-Life.* Translated by Adam Kotsko. Stanford: Stanford University Press, 2013.

3. ____. *Homo Sacer: Sovereign Power and Bare Life.* Translated by Daniel Heller-Roazen. Stanford: Stanford University Press, 1998.

4. ____. *State of Exception.* Translated by Kevin Attell. Chicago: University of Chicago Press, 2005.

5. Allen, Amy. "Foucault, Feminism and the Self: The Politics of Personal Transformation." In *Feminism and the Final Foucault,* edited by Dianna Taylor and Karen Vintges, 235–57. Chicago: University of Illinois Press, 2004.

6. Ball, Kelly H. "'More or Less Raped': Foucault, Causality, and Feminist Critiques of Sexual Violence." *philoSOPHIA* 3, no.1 (2013): 52–68.

7. Branaman, Ann. "Contemporary Social Theory and the Sociological Study of Mental Health." In *Mental Health, Social Mirror,* edited by William R. Avison, Jane D. McLeod and Bernice A. Pescosolido, 95–126. New York: Springer, 2007.

8. Bunton, Robin, and Alan Petersen, eds. *Foucault, Health and Medicine.* London: Routledge, 2002.

9. Butler, Judith. *Bodies That Matter.* London: Routledge, 1993.

10. ____. *Gender Trouble.* London: Routledge, 1990.

11. Carrette, Jeremy R. *Foucault and Religion: Spiritual Corporality and Political Spirituality.* London: Routledge, 2000.

12. Cavallaro, Dani. *French Feminist Theory: An Introduction.* London: Continuum, 2003.

13. Clark, Elizabeth A. "Foucault, The Fathers and Sex." *Journal of the American Academy of Religion* 56, no .4 (1988): 619–41.

14. Clifford, James. *The Predicament of Culture: Twentieth-Century Ethnography, Literature, and Art.* Cambridge, Mass: Harvard University Press, 1988.

15. Defert, Daniel. "Chronology." In *A Companion to Foucault*, edited by Christopher Falzon, Timothy O'Leary and Jana Sawicki. Chichester: Wiley & Sons, 2013.

16. Diamond, Irene, and Lee Quinby. *Feminism & Foucault: Reflections on Resistance.* Boston: Northeastern University Press, 1988.

17. Dosse, Francois. *History of Structuralism. Volume II. The Sign Sets 1967–Present.* Translated by Deborah Glassman. Minneapolis: University of Minnesota Press, 1998.

18. Dreyfus, Hubert, and Paul Rabinow, eds. *Michel Foucault: Beyond Structuralism and Hermeneutics.* Chicago: University of Chicago Press, 1983.

19. Foucault, Michel. *The Archaeology of Knowledge (and the Discourse on Language).* Translated by A. M. Sheridan-Smith. London: Tavistock Publications Limited, 1972.

20. ____. *The Birth of the Clinic: An Archaeology of Medical Perception.* Translated by A. M. Sheridan-Smith. London: Routledge, 2003.

21. ____. *Discipline and Punish: The Birth of the Prison.* Translated by Alan Sheridan-Smith. New York: Random House, 1977.

22. ____. "The Ethics of the Concern for Self as a Practice of Freedom." Translated by P. Aranaov and D. McGrawth. In *Michel Foucault: Ethics, Subjectivity and Truth*, edited by Paul Rabinow, 281–302. New York: The New Press, 1997.

23. ____. "La Folie Encirclé." *Change Collective* (Paris: 1977).

24. ____. *The History of Sexuality Vol. 1: The Will to Knowledge.* Translated by Robert Hurley. London: Penguin Books, 1998.

25. ____. *The History of Sexuality Vol. 2: The Use of Pleasure.* Translated by Robert Hurley. New York: Random House Digital, Inc., 2012.

26. ____. *The History of Sexuality Vol. 3: The Care of the Self.* Translated by Robert Hurley. New York: Random House Digital, Inc., 2012.

27. ____. *Madness and Civilization: A History of Insanity in the Age of Reason.* Translated by Richard Howard. London: Vintage, 2006.

28. ____. *The Order of Things: An Archaeology of the Human Sciences.* London: Routledge, 2001.

29. ____. *Power/knowledge: Selected Interviews and Other Writings: 1972–1977.* Edited by Colin Gordon. Translated by Colin Gordon, Leo Marshall, John Mepham and Kate Soper. New York: Random House, 1980.

30. ____. "Sexual Choice, Sexual Act." Translated by James O'Higgins. In *Michel Foucault: Ethics, Subjectivity and Truth*, edited by Paul Rabinow. New York: The New Press, 1997.

31. Fraser, Nancy. "From Discipline to Flexibilization? Rereading Foucault in the Shadow of Globalization," *Constellations* 10, no. 2 (2003): 160–71.

32. Halperin, David. *One Hundred Years of Homosexuality: and other Essays on Greek Love.* London: Routledge, 1990.

33. ____. *Saint Foucault: Towards a Gay Hagiography.* New York: Oxford University Press, 1995.

34. Hardt, Michael, and Antonio Negri. *Empire.* Cambridge: Harvard University Press, 2000.

35. Larmour, David H. J., Paul Allen and Charles Platter. "Situating the *History of Sexuality.*" In *Rethinking Sexuality: Foucault and Classical Antiquity,* edited by David H. J. Larmour, Paul Allen Miller, and Charles Platter, 3–41. Princeton, New Jersey: Princeton University Press, 1998.

36. Larner, Wendy. "Neo-liberalism: Policy, Ideology, Governmentality." *Studies in Political Economy* 63 (2000): 5–25.

37. Leonard, Diana, and Lisa Adkins. "Reconstructing French Feminism: Commodification, Materialism and Sex." In *Sex in Question: French Materialist Feminism*, edited by Diana Leonard and Lisa Adkins, 1–23. London: Taylor & Francis, 1996.

38. Macey, David. *The Lives of Michel Foucault.* New York: Pantheon, 1993.

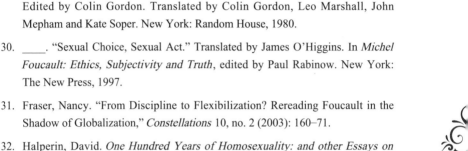

39. Marcuse, Herbert. *Eros and Civilization: A Philosophical Inquiry into Freud.* Boston: Beacon Press, 1974.

40. ____. *One-Dimensional Man: Studies in the Ideology of Advanced Industrial Society.* London: Routledge, 2002.

41. Martin, Biddy. "Feminism, Criticism, and Foucault." *New German Critique* 27 (1982): 3–30.

42. McWhorter, Ladelle. *Bodies and Pleasures: Foucault and the Politics of Sexual Normalization.* Bloomington: Indiana University Press, 1999.

43. Megill, Allan. "The Reception of Foucault by Historians." *Journal of the History of Ideas* 48 (1987): 117–41.

44. Nietzsche, Friedrich. *On the Genealogy of Morals and Ecce Homo.* New York: Random House, 2010 .

45. ____. *The Will to Power.* New York: Random House, 2011.

46. Nussbaum, Martha. "The Professor of Parody." *The New Republic* 22, no. 2 (1999): 37–45.

47. Plaza, Monique. "Our Costs and Their Benefits." In *Sex in Question: French Materialist Feminism*, edited by Diana Leonard and Lisa Adkins, 183–94. London: Taylor & Francis, 1996.

48. Poster, Mark. *Foucault, Marxism, and History: Mode of Production Versus Mode of Information.* Cambridge: Polity Press, 1984.

49. Rabinow, Paul. "Series Preface." In *Michel Foucault: Ethics, Subjectivity and Truth,* edited by Paul Rabinow. New York: The New Press, 1997.

50. Radden, Jennifer, ed. *The Philosophy of Psychiatry: A Companion.* Oxford: Oxford University Press, 2004.

51. Raulet, Gérard. "Structuralism and Post-structuralism: An Interview with Michel Foucault." *Telos* 55 (1983): 195–211. Accessed 16 October 2015. doi: 10.3817/0383055195.

52. Reich, Wilhelm. *The Mass Psychology of Fascism.* New York: Farrar, Straus & Giroux, 1970.

53. Roach, Thomas. "Sense and Sexuality: Foucault, Wojnarowicz, and Biopower." *Nebula: A Journal of Multidisciplinary Scholarship* 6, no. 3 (2009): 155–73.

54. Rogers, Ann, and David Pilgrim. *A Sociology of Mental Health and Illness.* Maidenhead: Open University Press.

55. Schrift, Alan D. *Nietzsche's French Legacy: A Genealogy of Poststructuralism.* London: Routledge, 1995.

56. Soper, Kate. "Productive Contradictions." In *Up Against Foucault: Explorations of Some Tensions Between Foucault and Feminism,* edited by Caroline Ramazanoglu, 29–51. New York: Routledge, 1993.

57. Spargo, Tamsin. *Foucault and Queer Theory.* Cambridge: Icon books, 1999.

58. Stoler, Ann Laura. *Race and the Education of Desire: Foucault's History of Sexuality and the Colonial Order of Things.* Durham, North Carolina: Duke University Press, 1995.

59. Stone, Nick. "The Foucauldian-Marxist Conflict: Exploitation and Power in Gay Marriage." *Discoveries* 7 (2006): 65–72. Accessed November 15, 2015. http: //www.arts.cornell.edu/knight_institute/publicationsprizes/discoveries/discoveriesspring2006/06stone.pdf.

60. Sullivan, Nikki. *A Critical Introduction to Queer Theory.* New York: NYU Press, 2003.

原书作者简介

米歇尔·福柯于 1926 年出生在法国一个富裕而保守的家庭。大学里他攻读哲学，但是当时社会对同性恋非常排斥，对身为同性恋的福柯造成很大影响。福柯在 20 多岁的时候自杀未遂，曾被关在一家精神病院接受治疗。福柯被公认为最重要的现代思想家之一。他对权力、知识和个体形成之间的相互作用进行了分析，对很多学术领域（包括社会学、历史和哲学）都做出了杰出贡献。福柯于 1984 年去世，享年 57 岁。

本书作者简介

拉凯莱·迪尼博士曾就读于剑桥大学、伦敦大学国王学院和伦敦大学学院。目前她的大部分作品都关注现代英美小说对生产和消费的呈现。她曾在剑桥大学和国际教育基金会任教，目前在罗汉普顿大学担任英语讲师。她的第一部专著《20 世纪小说中的消费主义、浪费和再利用：先锋派的遗产》由英国帕尔格雷夫·麦克米伦出版社于 2016 年出版。

克艾拉·布里甘蒂博士多年来担任卡尔顿学院英语文学和性别研究的教授，现在是伦敦国王学院的访问研究员。布里甘蒂博士是《国内现代主义、两次世界大战间的小说和艾米莉·希尔达·扬》和《国内空间解读》（多伦多大学出版社，2013）两部著作的合著者。

世界名著中的批判性思维

《世界思想宝库钥匙丛书》致力于深入浅出地阐释全世界著名思想家的观点，不论是谁、在何处都能了解到，从而推进批判性思维发展。

《世界思想宝库钥匙丛书》与世界顶尖大学的一流学者合作，为一系列学科中最有影响的著作推出新的分析文本，介绍其观点和影响。在这一不断扩展的系列中，每种选入的著作都代表了历经时间考验的思想典范。通过为这些著作提供必要背景、揭示原作者的学术渊源以及说明这些著作所产生的影响，本系列图书希望让读者以新视角看待这些划时代的经典之作。读者应学会思考、运用并挑战这些著作中的观点，而不是简单接受它们。

ABOUT THE AUTHOR OF THE ORIGINAL WORK

Michel Foucault was born in 1926 into a wealthy and conservative French family. He studied philosophy, but being gay in a homophobic society took its toll, and after a suicide attempt in his early 20s, he was treated in a psychiatric hospital. Foucault is considered one of the most important modern thinkers. His analyses of the interplay of power, knowledge, and the makeup of the individual are considered key contributions to a wide range of academic fields, including sociology, history, and philosophy. Foucault died in 1984 at the age of 57.

ABOUT THE AUTHORS OF THE ANALYSIS

Dr Rachele Dini studied at Cambridge, King's College London and University College London. Much of her current work focuses on the representation of production and consumption in modern and contemporary Anglo-American fiction. She has taught at Cambridge and for the Foundation for International Education, and is now Lecturer in English at the University of Roehampton. Her first monograph, *Consumerism, Waste and Re-use in Twentieth-century Fiction: Legacies of the Avant-Garde*, was published by Palgrave Macmillan in 2016.

Dr Chiara Briganti was a professor of English Literature and Gender Studies at Carleton College, for many years, and is now a visiting research fellow at King's College London. Dr Briganti is co-author of *Domestic Modernism, the Interwar Novel, and E. H. Young* and *The Domestic Space Reader* (University of Toronto Press, 2013).

ABOUT MACAT
GREAT WORKS FOR CRITICAL THINKING

Macat is focused on making the ideas of the world's great thinkers accessible and comprehensible to everybody, everywhere, in ways that promote the development of enhanced critical thinking skills.

It works with leading academics from the world's top universities to produce new analyses that focus on the ideas and the impact of the most influential works ever written across a wide variety of academic disciplines. Each of the works that sit at the heart of its growing library is an enduring example of great thinking. But by setting them in context — and looking at the influences that shaped their authors, as well as the responses they provoked — Macat encourages readers to look at these classics and game-changers with fresh eyes. Readers learn to think, engage and challenge their ideas, rather than simply accepting them.

批判性思维与《性史（第一卷）：求知意志》

首要批判性思维技巧：创造性思维

次要批判性思维技巧：阐释

　　米歇尔·福柯是 20 世纪最具创新性思维和涉猎最广泛的学者之一，这使得他成为作品被阅读次数最多和最具影响力的理论家之一，也在《性史》中得到了充分的体现。《性史》是福柯在 1984 年去世前完成的最后一部作品。

　　福柯的吸引力在于其思想的创造力。创造性思维有多种形式，从以新颖的方式重新定义某一问题，到在事物之间找到令人意想不到且具有启发性的联系。将问题完全颠覆的能力可能是福柯的特殊才能最完美的体现。例如关于性存在这一问题，通过对历史证据的解读，他认为我们习惯的性分类（同性恋、女同性恋、异性恋等）并不是"自然的"，而是权力和知识在社会中相互作用的结果。

　　福柯认为这样的分类实际上有助于促进分类所想要命名的欲望的形成。反过来，这些类别的产生，与社会对不同性别群体的权力作用密切相关。

　　福柯的思想虽然现在显得十分平常，但是在其产生的时代却是异常新颖、极具挑战性的。通过福柯的视点来看世界，就是要以一种截然不同的、极具启发性的方式来看待世界。这是创造性思维的一个最好的例证。

CRITICAL THINKING AND *THE HISTORY OF SEXUALITY VOL. 1*

- Primary critical thinking skill: CREATIVE THINKING
- Secondary critical thinking skill: INTERPRETATION

Michel Foucault is famous as one of the 20th-century's most innovative and wide-ranging thinkers. The qualities that made him one of the most-read and influential theorists of the modern age find full expression in *The History of Sexuality*, the last project Foucault was able to complete before his death in 1984.

Central to Foucault's appeal is the creativity of his thought. Creative thinking takes many forms — from redefining an issue in a novel way to making unexpected and illuminating connections. Foucault's particular talent could perhaps best be described as turning questions inside out. In the case of sexuality, for instance, his interpretation of the historical evidence led him to argue that the sexual categories that we are used to (homosexual, lesbian, straight, and so on) are not "natural," but constructs that are products of the ways in which power and knowledge interact in society.

Such categories, Foucault continues, actually serve to produce the desires they seek to name. And their creation, in turn, is closely linked to the power that society exerts on those who belong to different sexual groups.

Foucault's ideas — familiar now — were so novel in their time that they proved highly challenging. But to see the world through Foucault's thought is to see it in a profoundly different and illuminating way — an example of creative thinking at its best.

《世界思想宝库钥匙丛书》简介

《世界思想宝库钥匙丛书》致力于为一系列在各领域产生重大影响的人文社科类经典著作提供独特的学术探讨。每一本读物都不仅仅是原经典著作的内容摘要，而是介绍并深入研究原经典著作的学术渊源、主要观点和历史影响。这一丛书的目的是提供一套学习资料，以促进读者掌握批判性思维，从而更全面、深刻地去理解重要思想。

每一本读物分为 3 个部分：学术渊源、学术思想和学术影响，每个部分下有 4 个小节。这些章节旨在从各个方面研究原经典著作及其反响。

由于独特的体例，每一本读物不但易于阅读，而且另有一项优点：所有读物的编排体例相同，读者在进行某个知识层面的调查或研究时可交叉参阅多本该丛书中的相关读物，从而开启跨领域研究的路径。

为了方便阅读，每本读物最后还列出了术语表和人名表（在书中则以星号 * 标记），此外还有参考文献。

《世界思想宝库钥匙丛书》与剑桥大学合作，理清了批判性思维的要点，即如何通过 6 种技能来进行有效思考。其中 3 种技能让我们能够理解问题，另 3 种技能让我们有能力解决问题。这 6 种技能合称为"批判性思维 PACIER 模式"，它们是：

分析：了解如何建立一个观点；
评估：研究一个观点的优点和缺点；
阐释：对意义所产生的问题加以理解；
创造性思维：提出新的见解，发现新的联系；
解决问题：提出切实有效的解决办法；
理性化思维：创建有说服力的观点。

THE MACAT LIBRARY

The Macat Library is a series of unique academic explorations of seminal works in the humanities and social sciences — books and papers that have had a significant and widely recognised impact on their disciplines. It has been created to serve as much more than just a summary of what lies between the covers of a great book. It illuminates and explores the influences on, ideas of, and impact of that book. Our goal is to offer a learning resource that encourages critical thinking and fosters a better, deeper understanding of important ideas.

Each publication is divided into three Sections: Influences, Ideas, and Impact. Each Section has four Modules. These explore every important facet of the work, and the responses to it.

This Section-Module structure makes a Macat Library book easy to use, but it has another important feature. Because each Macat book is written to the same format, it is possible (and encouraged!) to cross-reference multiple Macat books along the same lines of inquiry or research. This allows the reader to open up interesting interdisciplinary pathways.

To further aid your reading, lists of glossary terms and people mentioned are included at the end of this book (these are indicated by an asterisk [*] throughout) — as well as a list of works cited.

Macat has worked with the University of Cambridge to identify the elements of critical thinking and understand the ways in which six different skills combine to enable effective thinking.

Three allow us to fully understand a problem; three more give us the tools to solve it. Together, these six skills make up the PACIER model of critical thinking. They are:

ANALYSIS — understanding how an argument is built
EVALUATION — exploring the strengths and weaknesses of an argument
INTERPRETATION — understanding issues of meaning
CREATIVE THINKING — coming up with new ideas and fresh connections
PROBLEM-SOLVING — producing strong solutions
REASONING — creating strong arguments

"《世界思想宝库钥匙丛书》提供了独一无二的跨学科学习和研究工具。它介绍那些革新了各自学科研究的经典著作，还邀请全世界一流专家和教育机构进行严谨的分析，为每位读者打开世界顶级教育的大门。"

—— 安德烈亚斯·施莱歇尔，
经济合作与发展组织教育与技能司司长

"《世界思想宝库钥匙丛书》直面大学教育的巨大挑战……他们组建了一支精干而活跃的学者队伍，来推出在研究广度上颇具新意的教学材料。"

—— 布罗尔斯教授、勋爵，剑桥大学前校长

"《世界思想宝库钥匙丛书》的愿景令人赞叹。它通过分析和阐释那些曾深刻影响人类思想以及社会、经济发展的经典文本，提供了新的学习方法。它推动批判性思维，这对于任何社会和经济体来说都是至关重要的。这就是未来的学习方法。"

—— 查尔斯·克拉克阁下，英国前教育大臣

"对于那些影响了各自领域的著作，《世界思想宝库钥匙丛书》能让人们立即了解到围绕那些著作展开的评论性言论，这让该系列图书成为在这些领域从事研究的师生们不可或缺的资源。"

—— 威廉·特朗佐教授，加利福尼亚大学圣地亚哥分校

"Macat offers an amazing first-of-its-kind tool for interdisciplinary learning and research. Its focus on works that transformed their disciplines and its rigorous approach, drawing on the world's leading experts and educational institutions, opens up a world-class education to anyone."

—— Andreas Schleicher, Director for Education and Skills, Organisation for Economic Co-operation and Development

"Macat is taking on some of the major challenges in university education... They have drawn together a strong team of active academics who are producing teaching materials that are novel in the breadth of their approach."

—— Prof Lord Broers, former Vice-Chancellor of the University of Cambridge

"The Macat vision is exceptionally exciting. It focuses upon new modes of learning which analyse and explain seminal texts which have profoundly influenced world thinking and so social and economic development. It promotes the kind of critical thinking which is essential for any society and economy. This is the learning of the future."

—— Rt Hon Charles Clarke, former UK Secretary of State for Education

"The Macat analyses provide immediate access to the critical conversation surrounding the books that have shaped their respective discipline, which will make them an invaluable resource to all of those, students and teachers, working in the field."

—— Prof William Tronzo, University of California at San Diego

TITLE	中文书名	类别
An Analysis of Arjun Appadurai's *Modernity at Large: Cultural Dimensions of Globalization*	解析阿尔君·阿帕杜莱《消失的现代性：全球化的文化维度》	人类学
An Analysis of Claude Lévi-Strauss's *Structural Anthropology*	解析克劳德·列维–斯特劳斯《结构人类学》	人类学
An Analysis of Marcel Mauss's *The Gift*	解析马塞尔·莫斯《礼物》	人类学
An Analysis of Jared M. Diamond's *Guns, Germs, and Steel: The Fate of Human Societies*	解析贾雷德·M.戴蒙德《枪炮、病菌与钢铁：人类社会的命运》	人类学
An Analysis of Clifford Geertz's *The Interpretation of Cultures*	解析克利福德·格尔茨《文化的解释》	人类学
An Analysis of Philippe Ariès's *Centuries of Childhood: A Social History of Family Life*	解析菲力浦·阿利埃斯《儿童的世纪：旧制度下的儿童和家庭生活》	人类学
An Analysis of W. Chan Kim & Renée Mauborgne's *Blue Ocean Strategy*	解析金伟灿/勒妮·莫博涅《蓝海战略》	商业
An Analysis of John P. Kotter's *Leading Change*	解析约翰·P.科特《领导变革》	商业
An Analysis of Michael E. Porter's *Competitive Strategy: Techniques for Analyzing Industries and Competitors*	解析迈克尔·E.波特《竞争战略：分析产业和竞争对手的技术》	商业
An Analysis of Jean Lave & Etienne Wenger's *Situated Learning: Legitimate Peripheral Participation*	解析琼·莱夫/艾蒂纳·温格《情境学习：合法的边缘性参与》	商业
An Analysis of Douglas McGregor's *The Human Side of Enterprise*	解析道格拉斯·麦格雷戈《企业的人性面》	商业
An Analysis of Milton Friedman's *Capitalism and Freedom*	解析米尔顿·弗里德曼《资本主义与自由》	商业
An Analysis of Ludwig von Mises's *The Theory of Money and Credit*	解析路德维希·冯·米塞斯《货币和信用理论》	经济学
An Analysis of Adam Smith's *The Wealth of Nations*	解析亚当·斯密《国富论》	经济学
An Analysis of Thomas Piketty's *Capital in the Twenty-First Century*	解析托马斯·皮凯蒂《21世纪资本论》	经济学
An Analysis of Nassim Nicholas Taleb's *The Black Swan: The Impact of the Highly Improbable*	解析纳西姆·尼古拉斯·塔勒布《黑天鹅：如何应对不可预知的未来》	经济学
An Analysis of Ha-Joon Chang's *Kicking Away the Ladder*	解析张夏准《富国陷阱：发达国家为何踢开梯子》	经济学
An Analysis of Thomas Robert Malthus's *An Essay on the Principle of Population*	解析托马斯·罗伯特·马尔萨斯《人口论》	经济学

An Analysis of John Maynard Keynes's *The General Theory of Employment, Interest and Money*	解析约翰·梅纳德·凯恩斯《就业、利息和货币通论》	经济学
An Analysis of Milton Friedman's *The Role of Monetary Policy*	解析米尔顿·弗里德曼《货币政策的作用》	经济学
An Analysis of Burton G. Malkiel's *A Random Walk Down Wall Street*	解析伯顿·G.马尔基尔《漫步华尔街》	经济学
An Analysis of Friedrich A. Hayek's *The Road to Serfdom*	解析弗里德里希·A.哈耶克《通往奴役之路》	经济学
An Analysis of Charles P. Kindleberger's *Manias, Panics, and Crashes: A History of Financial Crises*	解析查尔斯·P.金德尔伯格《疯狂、惊恐和崩溃：金融危机史》	经济学
An Analysis of Amartya Sen's *Development as Freedom*	解析阿马蒂亚·森《以自由看待发展》	经济学
An Analysis of Rachel Carson's *Silent Spring*	解析蕾切尔·卡森《寂静的春天》	地理学
An Analysis of Charles Darwin's *On the Origin of Species: by Means of Natural Selection, or The Preservation of Favoured Races in the Struggle for Life*	解析查尔斯·达尔文《物种起源》	地理学
An Analysis of World Commission on Environment and Development's *The Brundtland Report: Our Common Future*	解析世界环境与发展委员会《布伦特兰报告：我们共同的未来》	地理学
An Analysis of James E. Lovelock's *Gaia: A New Look at Life on Earth*	解析詹姆斯·E.拉伍洛克《盖娅：地球生命的新视野》	地理学
An Analysis of Paul Kennedy's *The Rise and Fall of the Great Powers: Economic Change and Military Conflict from 1500–2000*	解析保罗·肯尼迪《大国的兴衰：1500—2000年的经济变革与军事冲突》	历史
An Analysis of Janet L. Abu-Lughod's *Before European Hegemony: The World System A. D. 1250–1350*	解析珍妮特·L.阿布-卢格霍德《欧洲霸权之前：1250—1350年的世界体系》	历史
An Analysis of Alfred W. Crosby's *The Columbian Exchange: Biological and Cultural Consequences of 1492*	解析艾尔弗雷德·W.克罗斯比《哥伦布大交换：1492年以后的生物影响和文化冲击》	历史
An Analysis of Tony Judt's *Postwar: A History of Europe since 1945*	解析托尼·朱特《战后欧洲史》	历史
An Analysis of Richard J. Evans's *In Defence of History*	解析理查德·J.艾文斯《捍卫历史》	历史
An Analysis of Eric Hobsbawm's *The Age of Revolution: Europe 1789–1848*	解析艾瑞克·霍布斯鲍姆《革命的年代：欧洲1789—1848年》	历史

An Analysis of Roland Barthes's *Mythologies*	解析罗兰·巴特《神话学》	文学与批判理论
An Analysis of Simone de Beauvoir's *The Second Sex*	解析西蒙娜·德·波伏娃《第二性》	文学与批判理论
An Analysis of Edward W. Said's *Orientalism*	解析爱德华·W. 萨义德《东方主义》	文学与批判理论
An Analysis of Virginia Woolf's *A Room of One's Own*	解析弗吉尼亚·伍尔芙《一间自己的房间》	文学与批判理论
An Analysis of Judith Butler's *Gender Trouble*	解析朱迪斯·巴特勒《性别麻烦》	文学与批判理论
An Analysis of Ferdinand de Saussure's *Course in General Linguistics*	解析费尔迪南·德·索绪尔《普通语言学教程》	文学与批判理论
An Analysis of Susan Sontag's *On Photography*	解析苏珊·桑塔格《论摄影》	文学与批判理论
An Analysis of Walter Benjamin's *The Work of Art in the Age of Mechanical Reproduction*	解析瓦尔特·本雅明《机械复制时代的艺术作品》	文学与批判理论
An Analysis of W. E. B. Du Bois's *The Souls of Black Folk*	解析 W.E.B. 杜波依斯《黑人的灵魂》	文学与批判理论
An Analysis of Plato's *The Republic*	解析柏拉图《理想国》	哲学
An Analysis of Plato's *Symposium*	解析柏拉图《会饮篇》	哲学
An Analysis of Aristotle's *Metaphysics*	解析亚里士多德《形而上学》	哲学
An Analysis of Aristotle's *Nicomachean Ethics*	解析亚里士多德《尼各马可伦理学》	哲学
An Analysis of Immanuel Kant's *Critique of Pure Reason*	解析伊曼努尔·康德《纯粹理性批判》	哲学
An Analysis of Ludwig Wittgenstein's *Philosophical Investigations*	解析路德维希·维特根斯坦《哲学研究》	哲学
An Analysis of G. W. F. Hegel's *Phenomenology of Spirit*	解析 G.W.F. 黑格尔《精神现象学》	哲学
An Analysis of Baruch Spinoza's *Ethics*	解析巴鲁赫·斯宾诺莎《伦理学》	哲学
An Analysis of Hannah Arendt's *The Human Condition*	解析汉娜·阿伦特《人的境况》	哲学
An Analysis of G. E. M. Anscombe's *Modern Moral Philosophy*	解析 G.E.M. 安斯康姆《现代道德哲学》	哲学
An Analysis of David Hume's *An Enquiry Concerning Human Understanding*	解析大卫·休谟《人类理解研究》	哲学

An Analysis of Søren Kierkegaard's *Fear and Trembling*	解析索伦·克尔凯郭尔《恐惧与战栗》	哲学
An Analysis of René Descartes's *Meditations on First Philosophy*	解析勒内·笛卡尔《第一哲学沉思录》	哲学
An Analysis of Friedrich Nietzsche's *On the Genealogy of Morality*	解析弗里德里希·尼采《论道德的谱系》	哲学
An Analysis of Gilbert Ryle's *The Concept of Mind*	解析吉尔伯特·赖尔《心的概念》	哲学
An Analysis of Thomas Kuhn's *The Structure of Scientific Revolutions*	解析托马斯·库恩《科学革命的结构》	哲学
An Analysis of John Stuart Mill's *Utilitarianism*	解析约翰·斯图亚特·穆勒《功利主义》	哲学
An Analysis of Aristotle's *Politics*	解析亚里士多德《政治学》	政治学
An Analysis of Niccolò Machiavelli's *The Prince*	解析尼科洛·马基雅维利《君主论》	政治学
An Analysis of Karl Marx's *Capital*	解析卡尔·马克思《资本论》	政治学
An Analysis of Benedict Anderson's *Imagined Communities*	解析本尼迪克特·安德森《想象的共同体》	政治学
An Analysis of Samuel P. Huntington's *The Clash of Civilizations and the Remaking of World Order*	解析塞缪尔·P.亨廷顿《文明的冲突与世界秩序的重建》	政治学
An Analysis of Alexis de Tocqueville's *Democracy in America*	解析阿列克西·德·托克维尔《论美国的民主》	政治学
An Analysis of John A. Hobson's *Imperialism: A Study*	解析约翰·A.霍布森《帝国主义》	政治学
An Analysis of Thomas Paine's *Common Sense*	解析托马斯·潘恩《常识》	政治学
An Analysis of John Rawls's *A Theory of Justice*	解析约翰·罗尔斯《正义论》	政治学
An Analysis of Francis Fukuyama's *The End of History and the Last Man*	解析弗朗西斯·福山《历史的终结与最后的人》	政治学
An Analysis of John Locke's *Two Treatises of Government*	解析约翰·洛克《政府论》	政治学
An Analysis of Sun Tzu's *The Art of War*	解析孙武《孙子兵法》	政治学
An Analysis of Henry Kissinger's *World Order: Reflections on the Character of Nations and the Course of History*	解析亨利·基辛格《世界秩序》	政治学
An Analysis of Jean-Jacques Rousseau's *The Social Contract*	解析让-雅克·卢梭《社会契约论》	政治学

An Analysis of Odd Arne Westad's *The Global Cold War: Third World Interventions and the Making of Our Times*	解析文安立《全球冷战：美苏对第三世界的干涉与当代世界的形成》	政治学
An Analysis of Sigmund Freud's *The Interpretation of Dreams*	解析西格蒙德·弗洛伊德《梦的解析》	心理学
An Analysis of William James' *The Principles of Psychology*	解析威廉·詹姆斯《心理学原理》	心理学
An Analysis of Philip Zimbardo's *The Lucifer Effect*	解析菲利普·津巴多《路西法效应》	心理学
An Analysis of Leon Festinger's *A Theory of Cognitive Dissonance*	解析利昂·费斯汀格《认知失调论》	心理学
An Analysis of Richard H. Thaler & Cass R. Sunstein's *Nudge: Improving Decisions about Health, Wealth, and Happiness*	解析理查德·H.泰勒/卡斯·R.桑斯坦《助推：如何做出有关健康、财富和幸福的更优决策》	心理学
An Analysis of Gordon Allport's *The Nature of Prejudice*	解析高尔登·奥尔波特《偏见的本质》	心理学
An Analysis of Steven Pinker's *The Better Angels of Our Nature: Why Violence Has Declined*	解析斯蒂芬·平克《人性中的善良天使：暴力为什么会减少》	心理学
An Analysis of Stanley Milgram's *Obedience to Authority*	解析斯坦利·米尔格拉姆《对权威的服从》	心理学
An Analysis of Betty Friedan's *The Feminine Mystique*	解析贝蒂·弗里丹《女性的奥秘》	心理学
An Analysis of David Riesman *The Lonely Crowd: A Study of the Changing American Character*	解析大卫·理斯曼《孤独的人群：美国人社会性格演变之研究》	社会学
An Analysis of Franz Boas's *Race, Language and Culture*	解析弗朗兹·博厄斯《种族、语言与文化》	社会学
An Analysis of Pierre Bourdieu's *Outline of a Theory of Practice*	解析皮埃尔·布尔迪厄《实践理论大纲》	社会学
An Analysis of Max Weber's *The Protestant Ethic and the Spirit of Capitalism*	解析马克斯·韦伯《新教伦理与资本主义精神》	社会学
An Analysis of Jane Jacobs's *The Death and Life of Great American Cities*	解析简·雅各布斯《美国大城市的死与生》	社会学
An Analysis of C. Wright Mills's *The Sociological Imagination*	解析C.赖特·米尔斯《社会学的想象力》	社会学
An Analysis of Robert E. Lucas Jr.'s *Why Doesn't Capital Flow from Rich to Poor Countries?*	解析小罗伯特·E.卢卡斯《为何资本不从富国流向穷国？》	社会学

An Analysis of Émile Durkheim's *On Suicide*	解析埃米尔·迪尔凯姆《自杀论》	社会学
An Analysis of Eric Hoffer's *The True Believer: Thoughts on the Nature of Mass Movements*	解析埃里克·霍弗《狂热分子：群众运动圣经》	社会学
An Analysis of Jared M. Diamond's *Collapse: How Societies Choose to Fail or Survive*	解析贾雷德·M.戴蒙德《大崩溃：社会如何选择兴亡》	社会学
An Analysis of Michel Foucault's *The History of Sexuality Vol. 1: The Will to Knowledge*	解析米歇尔·福柯《性史（第一卷）：求知意志》	社会学
An Analysis of Michel Foucault's *Discipline and Punish*	解析米歇尔·福柯《规训与惩罚》	社会学
An Analysis of Richard Dawkins's *The Selfish Gene*	解析理查德·道金斯《自私的基因》	社会学
An Analysis of Antonio Gramsci's *Prison Notebooks*	解析安东尼奥·葛兰西《狱中札记》	社会学
An Analysis of Augustine's *Confessions*	解析奥古斯丁《忏悔录》	神学
An Analysis of C. S. Lewis's *The Abolition of Man*	解析C.S.路易斯《人之废》	神学

图书在版编目（CIP）数据

解析米歇尔·福柯《性史（第一卷）：求知意志》：汉、英 / 拉凯莱·迪尼（Rachele Dini），克艾拉·布里甘蒂（Chiara Briganti）著；苗绘译. —上海：上海外语教育出版社，2020
（世界思想宝库钥匙丛书）
ISBN 978-7-5446-6449-3

Ⅰ.①解⋯ Ⅱ.①拉⋯ ②克⋯ ③苗⋯ Ⅲ.①性学－研究－汉、英 Ⅳ.①C913.14

中国版本图书馆CIP数据核字（2020）第077922号

This Chinese-English bilingual edition of *An Analysis of Michel Foucault's* The History of Sexuality Vol. 1 The Will to Knowledge is published by arrangement with MACAT International Limited. Licensed for sale throughout the world.

本书汉英双语版由Macat国际有限公司授权上海外语教育出版社有限公司出版。供在全世界范围内发行、销售。

图字：09 – 2018 – 549

出版发行：**上海外语教育出版社**
　　　　　　（上海外国语大学内）　邮编：200083
电　　话：021-65425300（总机）
电子邮箱：bookinfo@sflep.com.cn
网　　址：http://www.sflep.com
责任编辑：梁瀚杰

印　　刷：上海信老印刷厂
开　　本：890×1240　1/32　印张 6.5　字数 134千字
版　　次：2020 年 11 月第 1 版　2020 年 11 月第 1 次印刷
印　　数：2 100 册

书　　号：ISBN 978-7-5446-6449-3
定　　价：30.00 元
本版图书如有印装质量问题，可向本社调换
质量服务热线：4008-213-263　电子邮箱：editorial@sflep.com